I'M AT THE END OF MY ROPE AND YOU'RE TUGGING AT IT.

Cartoons for People who Love Horses

JARED LEE

RED PONY™
PRESS

JARED LEE STUDIO

This book is dedicated to
Vernon "Sarge" Maddux –
war hero, pony exhibitor,
and special friend.

– JARED LEE

Printed in the United States of America

First Printing: April 2004

Second Printing: March 2005

Library of Congress Catalog Card Number Pending

ISBN 0-9677378-1-8

RED PONY™
P R E S S

A Division of Jared Lee Studio, Inc.
www.jaredlee.com

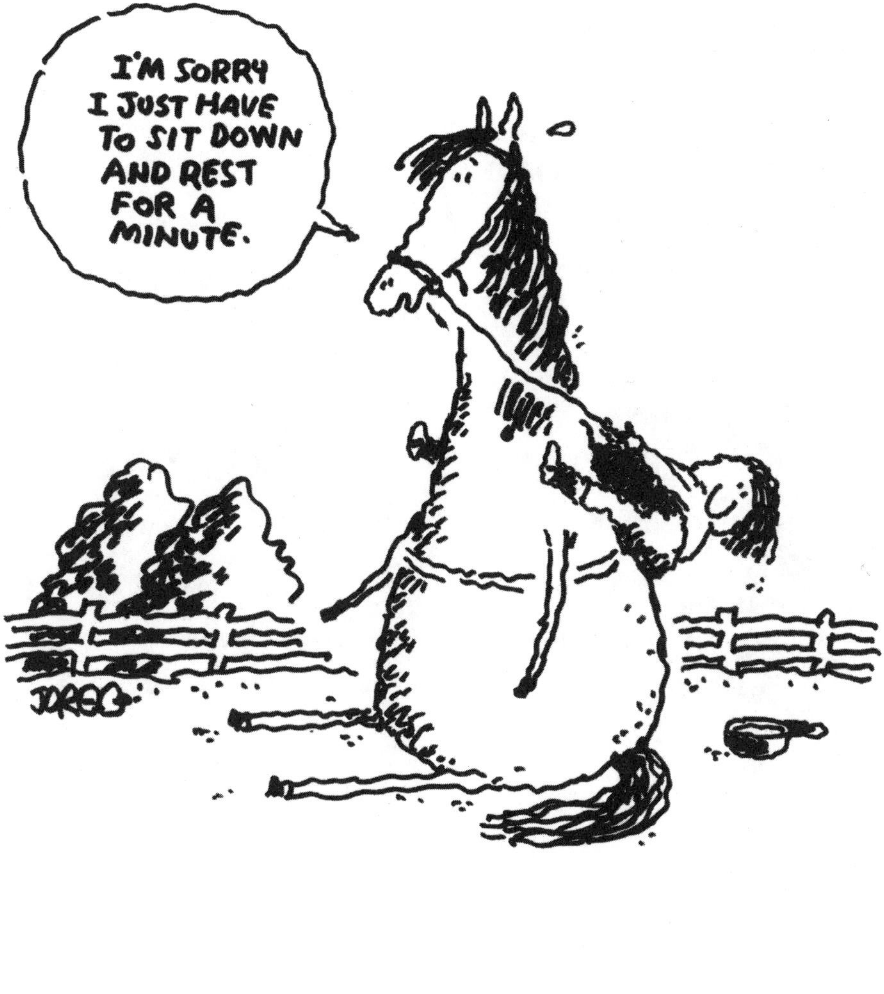
I'M SORRY I JUST HAVE TO SIT DOWN AND REST FOR A MINUTE.
JOREG

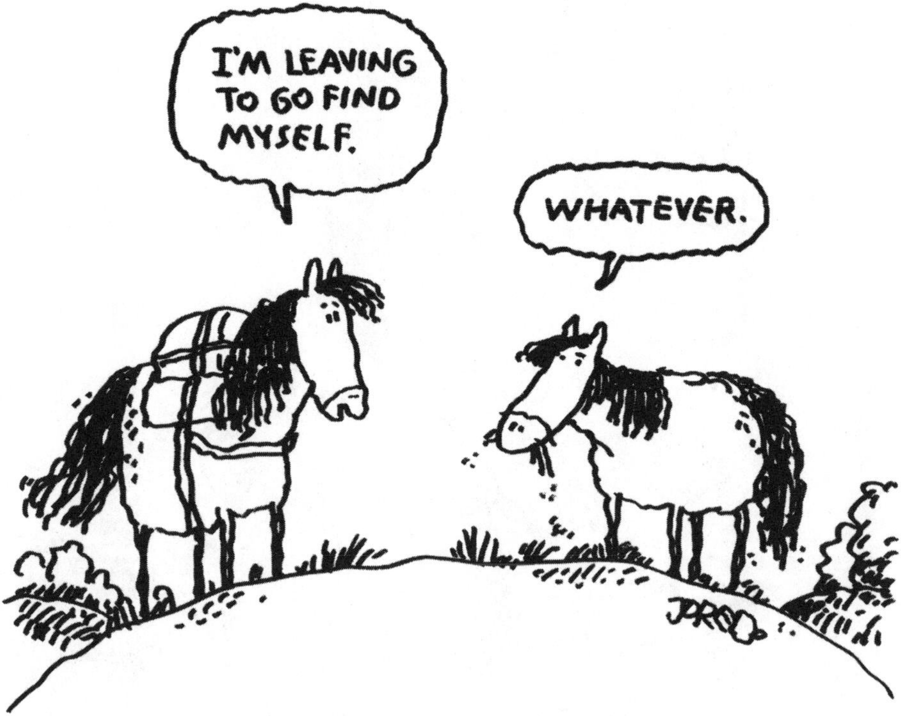
I'M LEAVING TO GO FIND MYSELF.
WHATEVER.
JARED

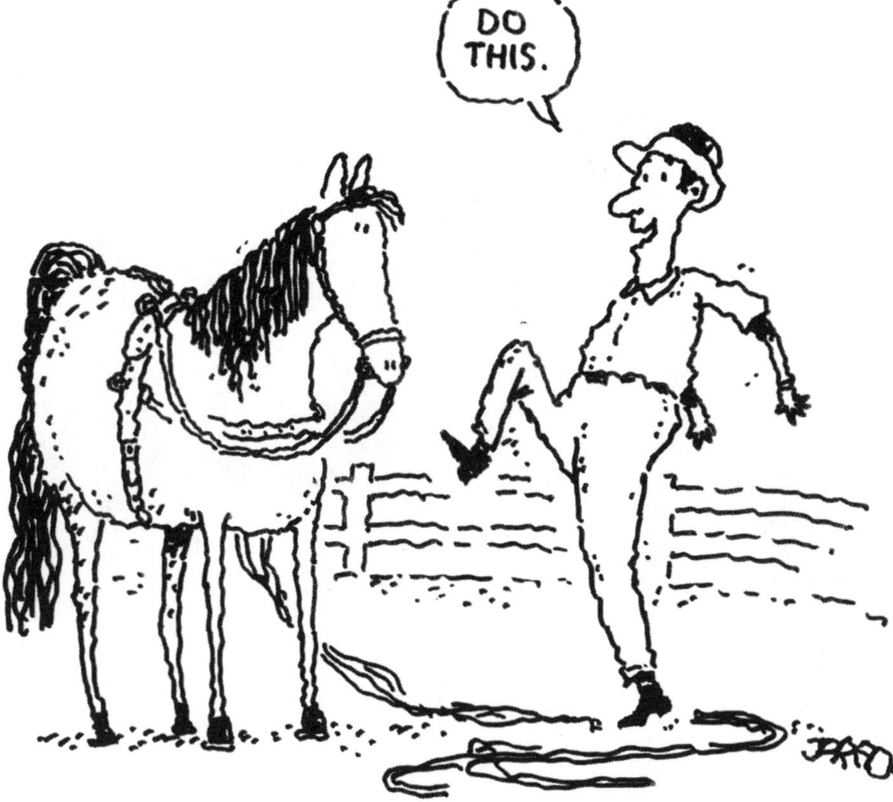
DO THIS.

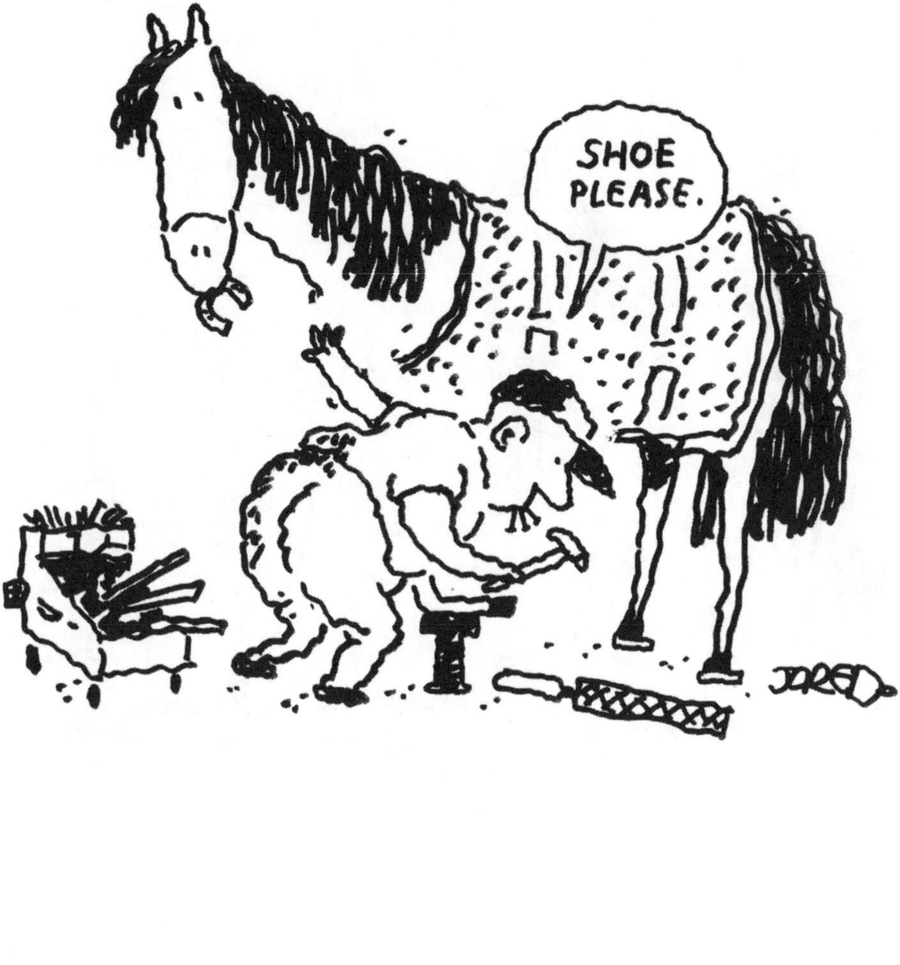
SHOE PLEASE.
JARED

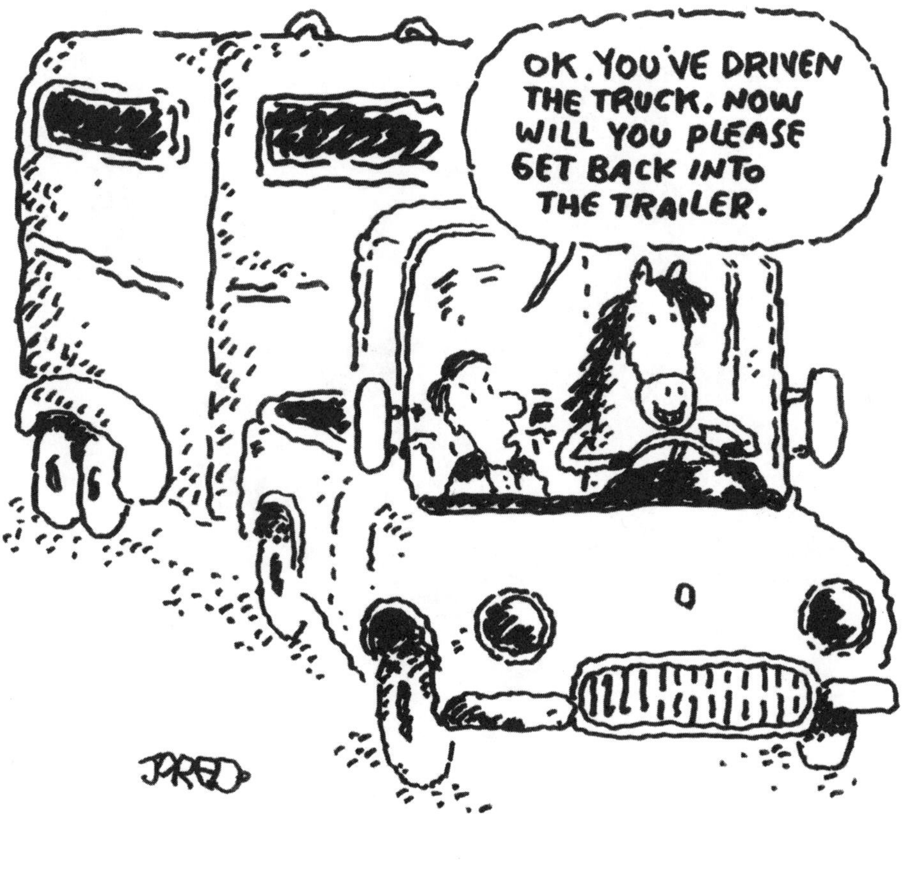
OK. YOU'VE DRIVEN THE TRUCK. NOW WILL YOU PLEASE GET BACK INTO THE TRAILER.
JARED

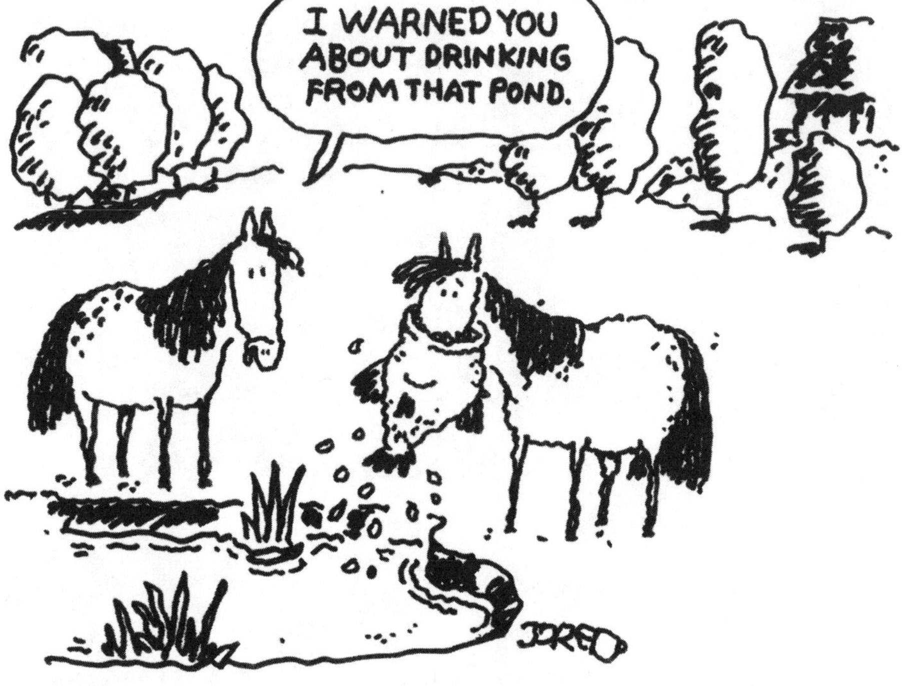
I WARNED YOU ABOUT DRINKING FROM THAT POND.

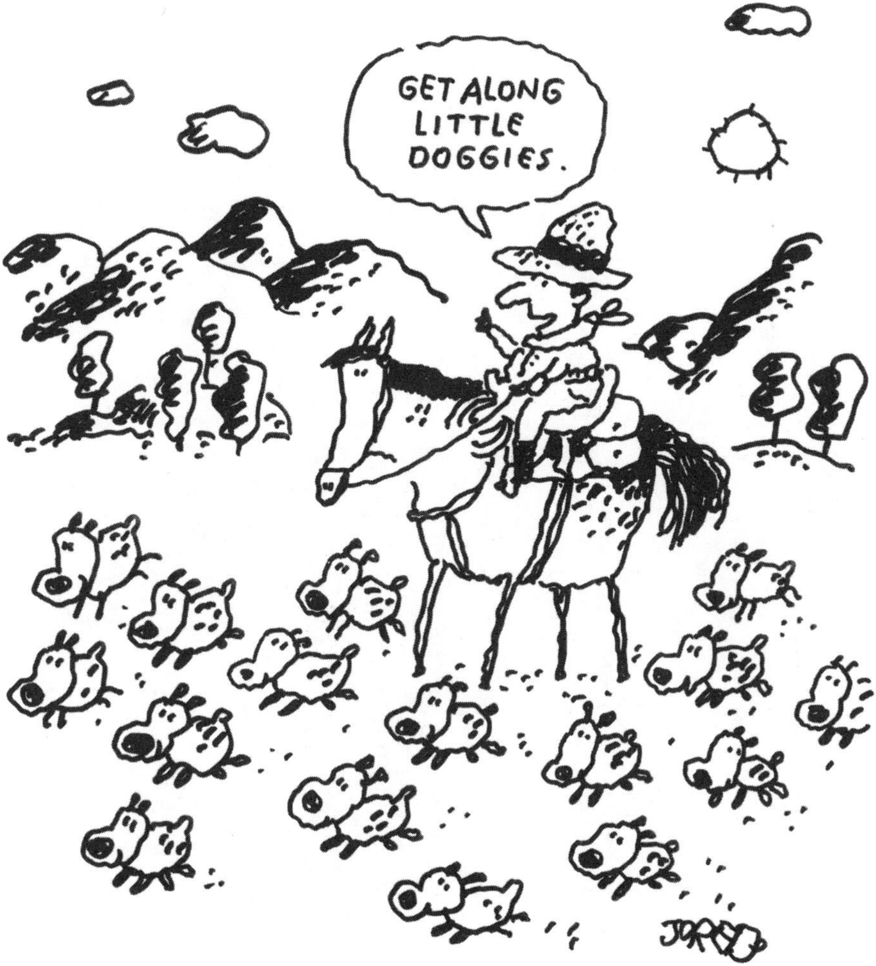
GET ALONG LITTLE DOGGIES.
JORGE

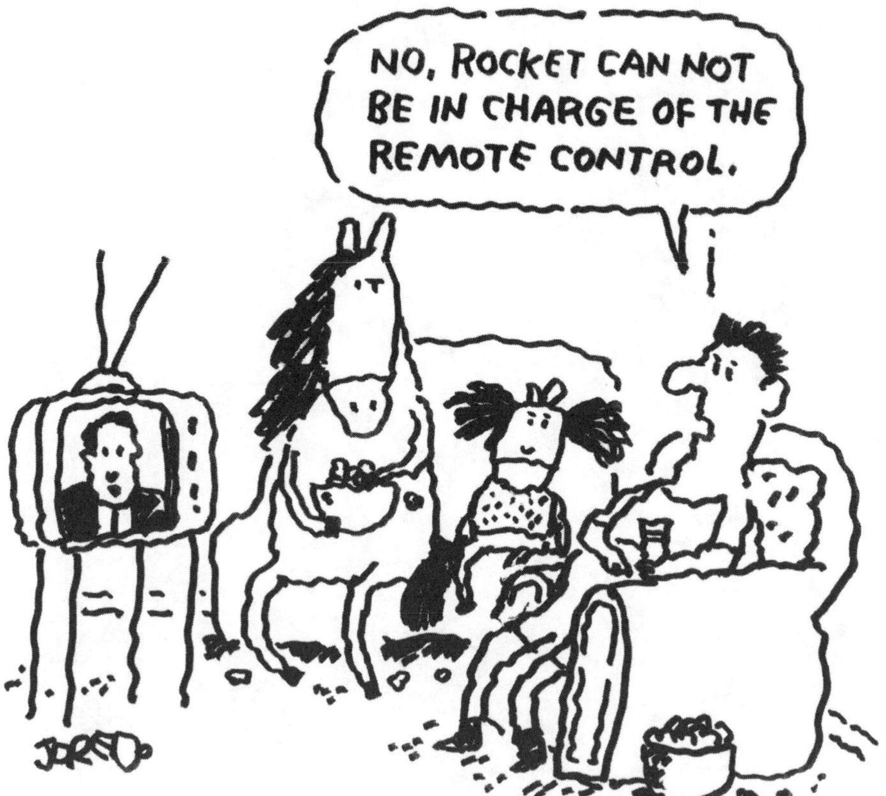
NO, ROCKET CAN NOT BE IN CHARGE OF THE REMOTE CONTROL.
JORED

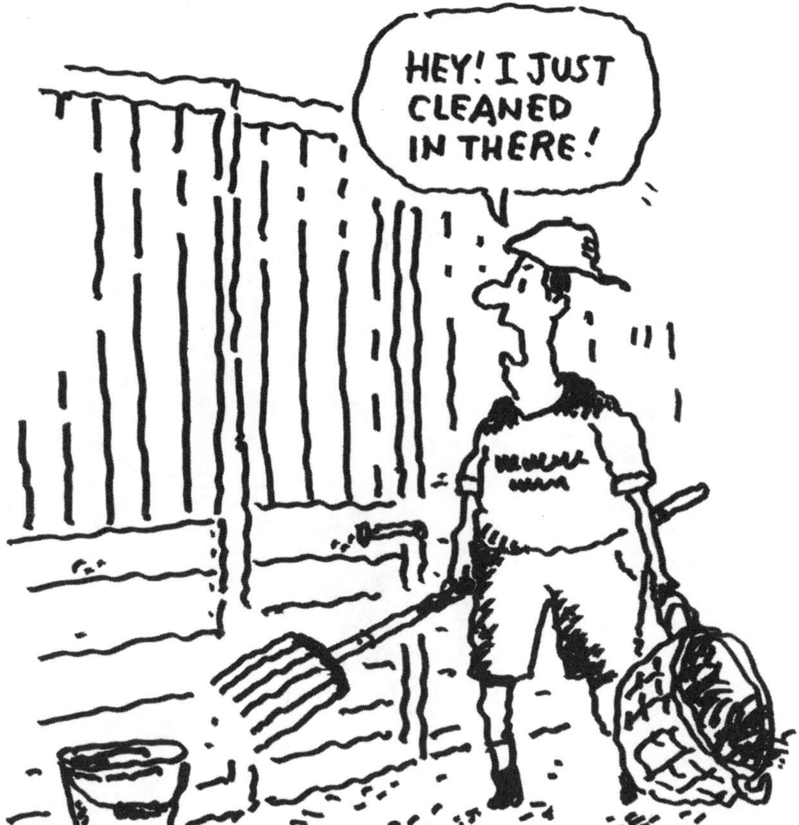
HEY! I JUST CLEANED IN THERE!

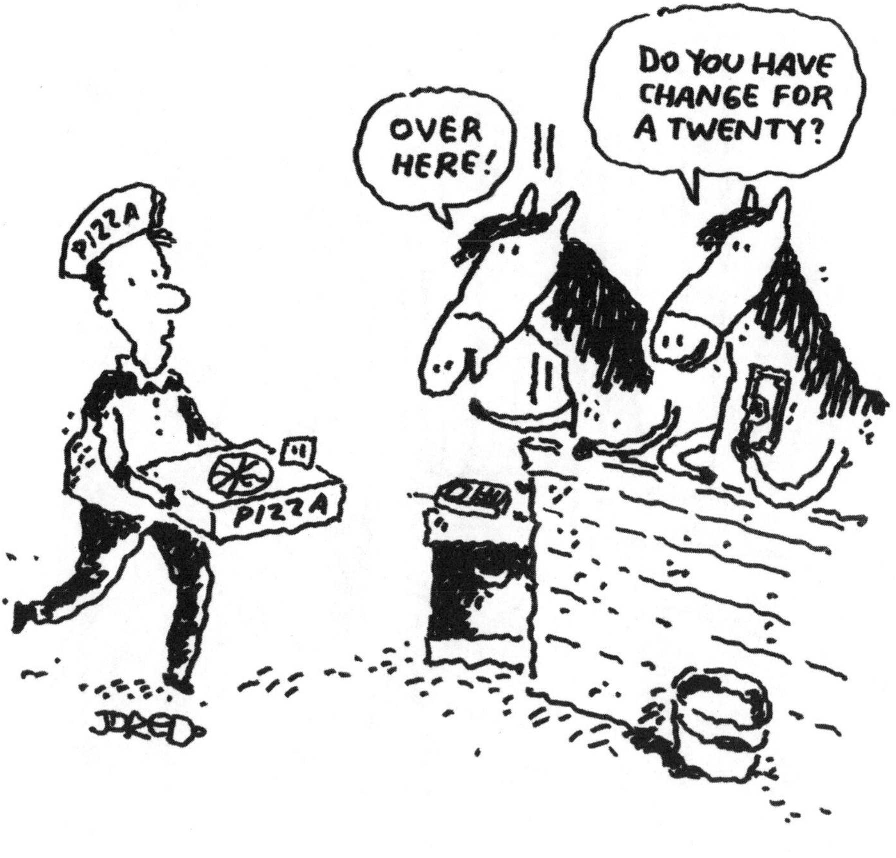
OVER HERE!
DO YOU HAVE CHANGE FOR A TWENTY?
PIZZA
PIZZA
JDRED

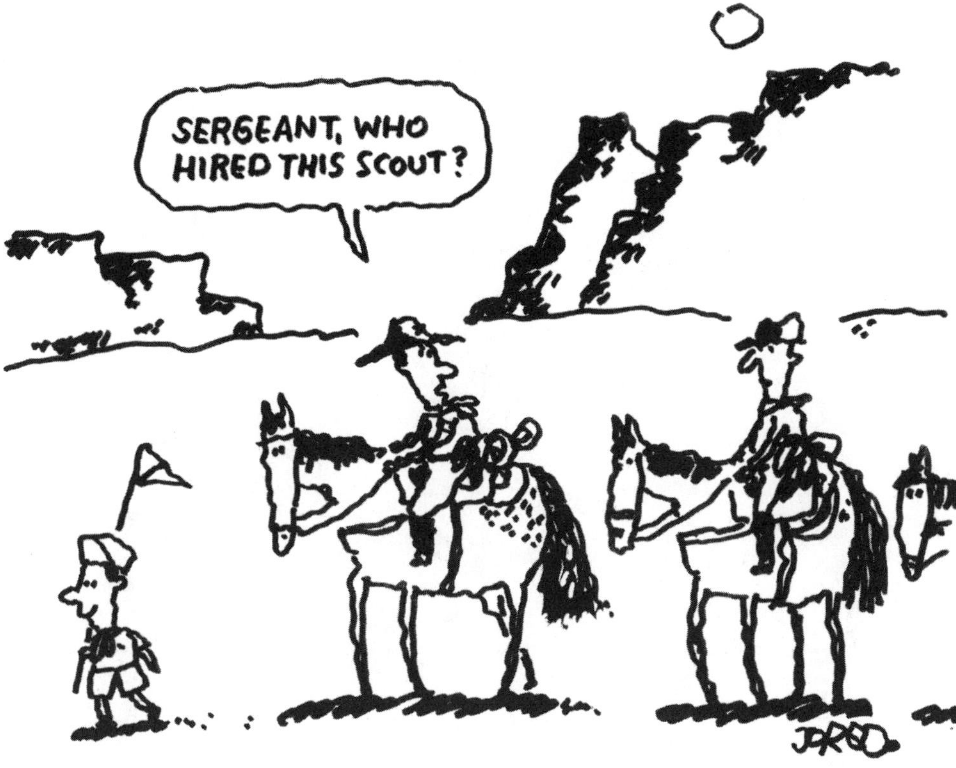
SERGEANT, WHO HIRED THIS SCOUT?
JORED

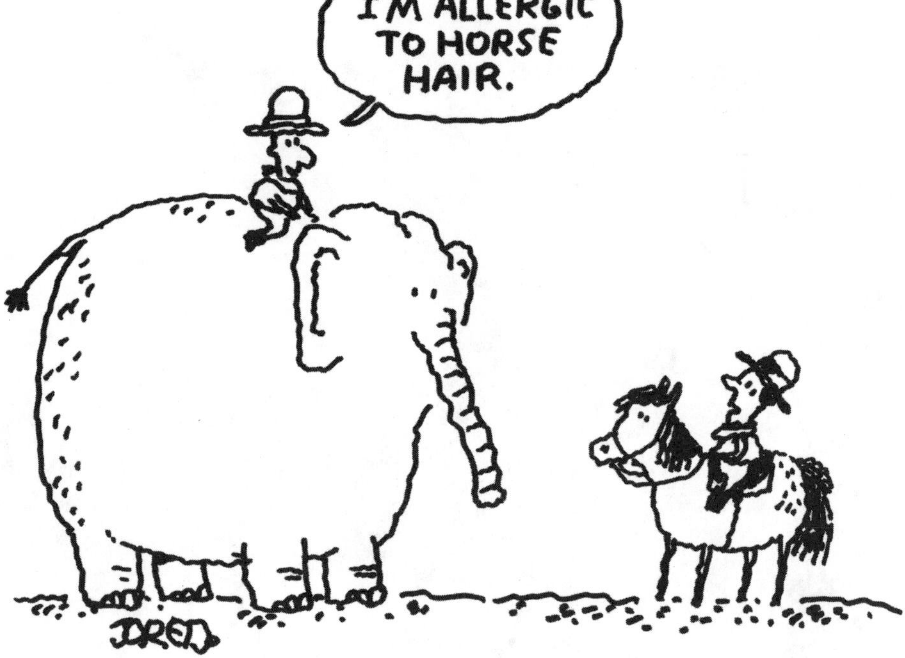
I'M ALLERGIC TO HORSE HAIR.
DRED

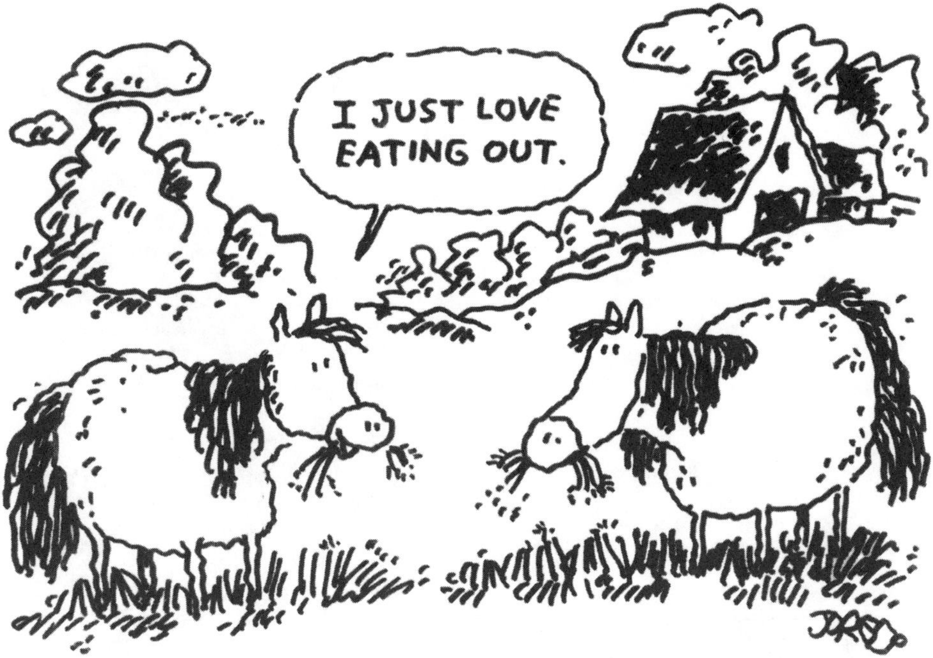
I JUST LOVE EATING OUT.

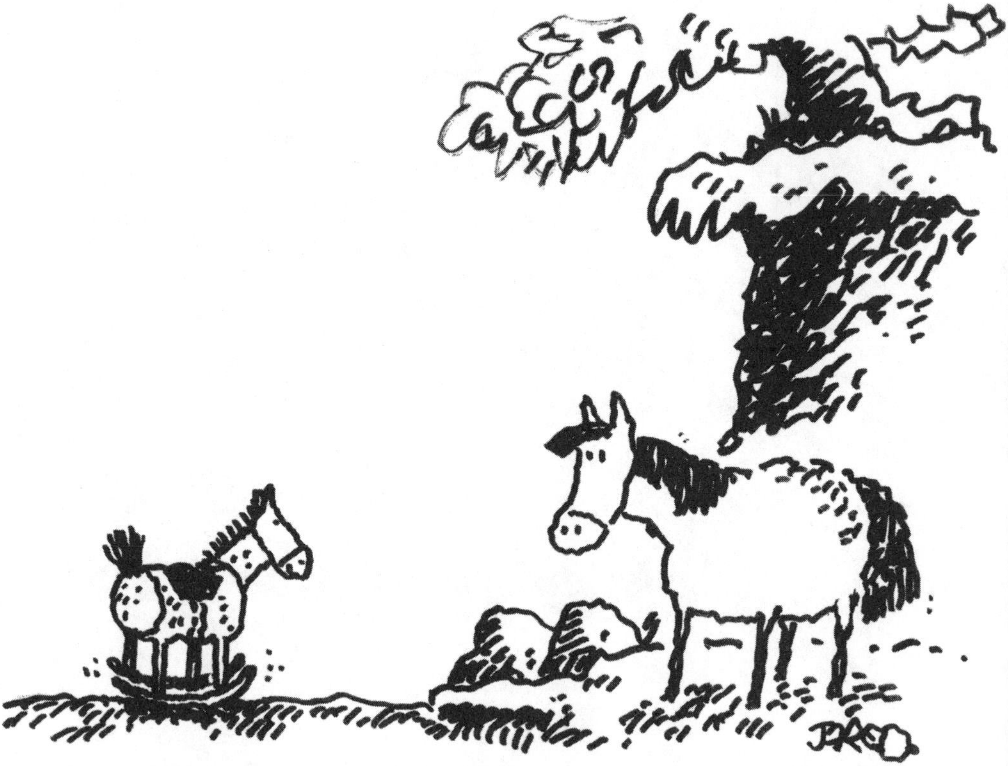

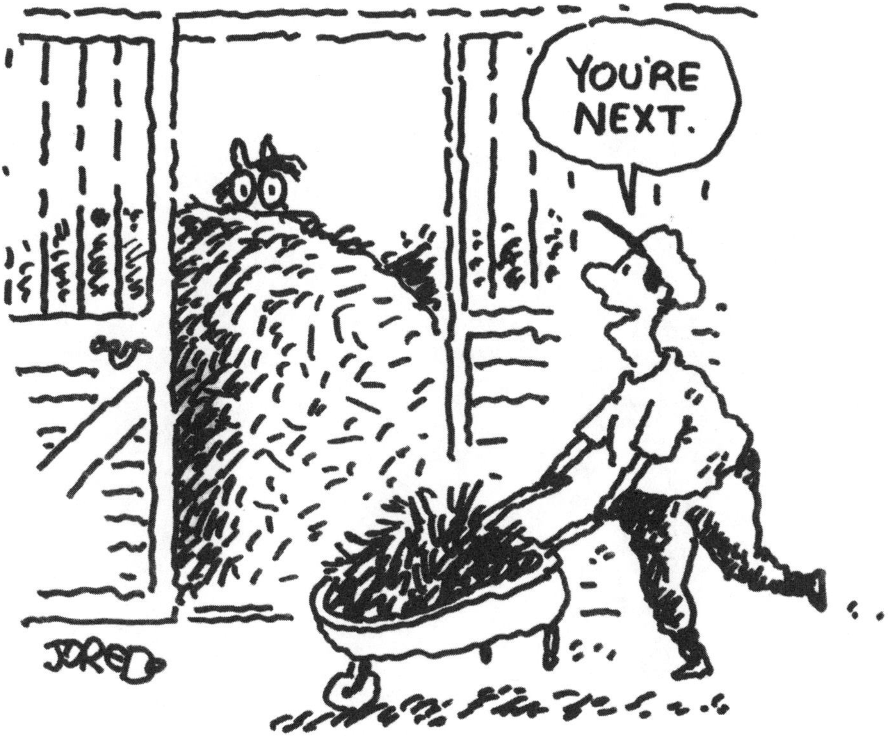
YOU'RE NEXT.
JARED

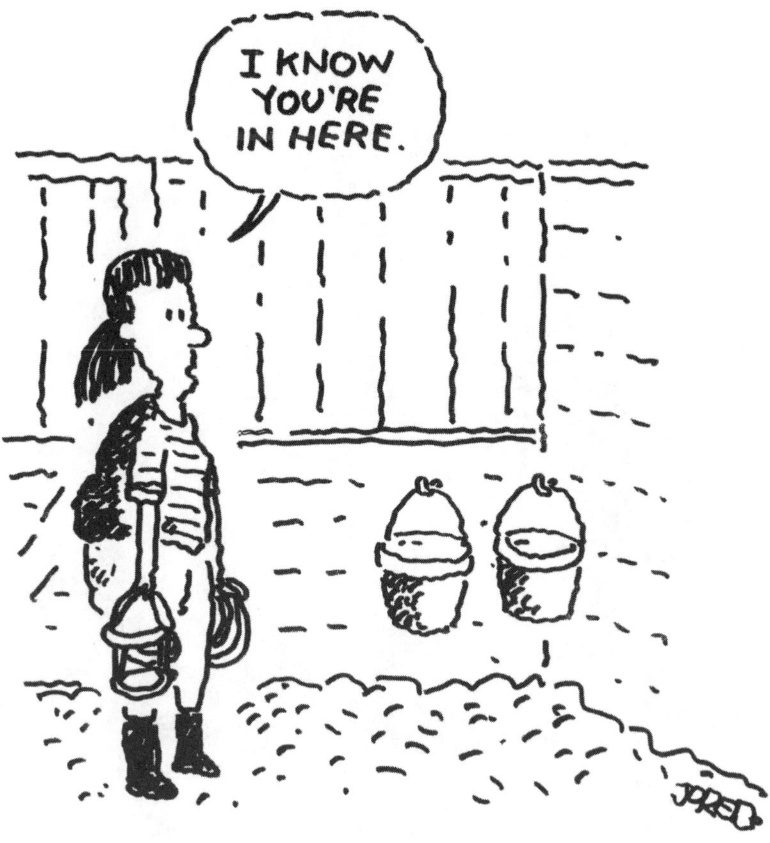
I KNOW YOU'RE IN HERE.

ELIZABETH THE INVISIBLE PONY

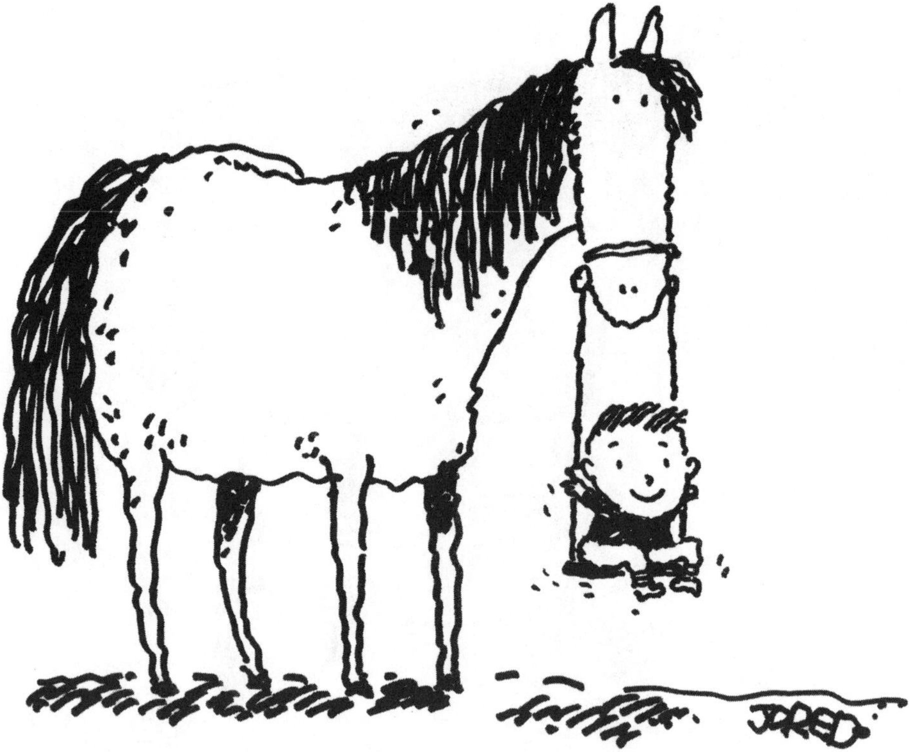
JARED

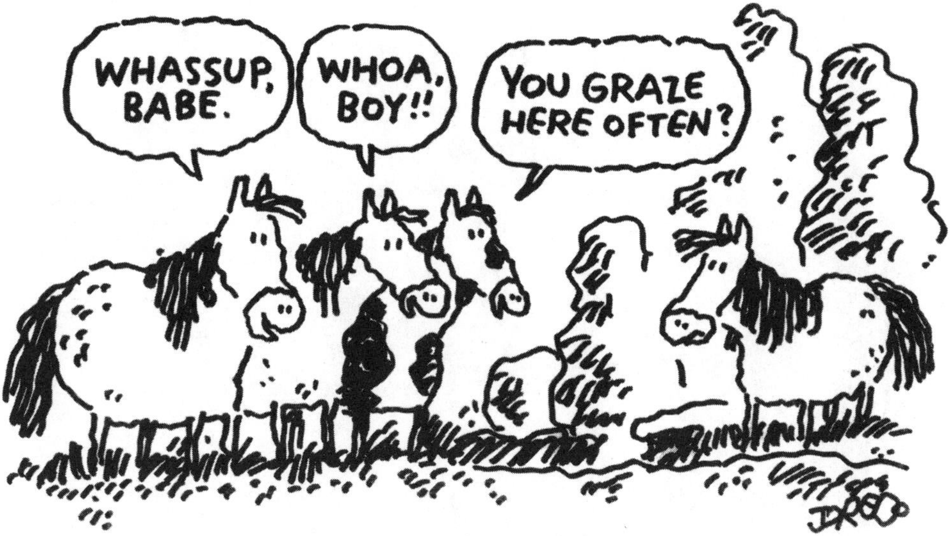
WHASSUP, BABE.
WHOA, BOY!!
YOU GRAZE HERE OFTEN?

FRESH HORSES

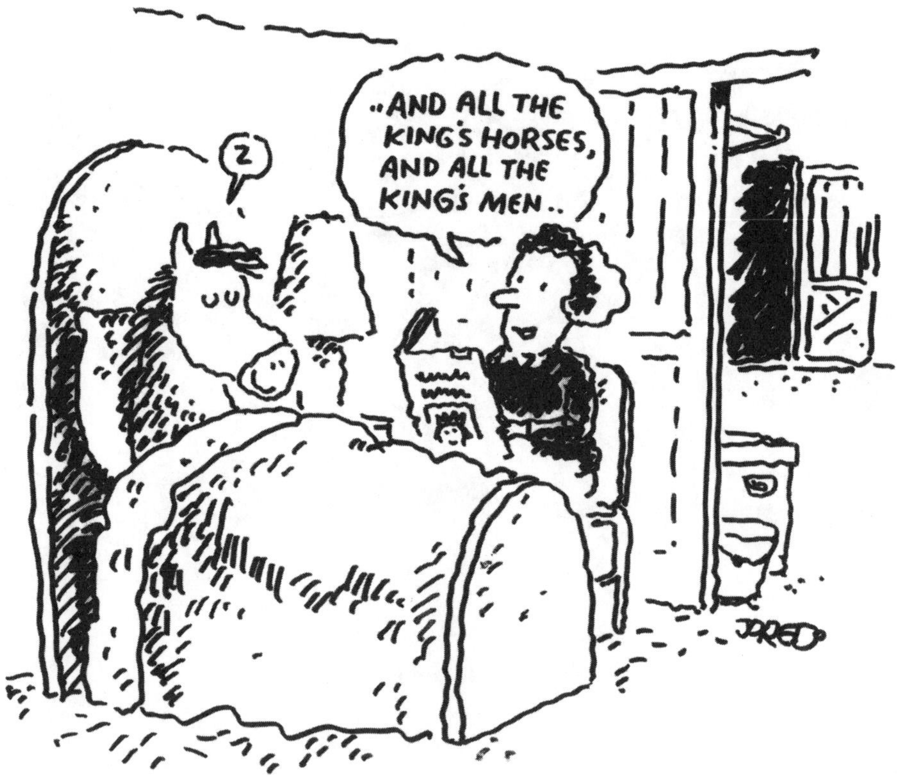
Z
..AND ALL THE KING'S HORSES, AND ALL THE KING'S MEN..
JARED

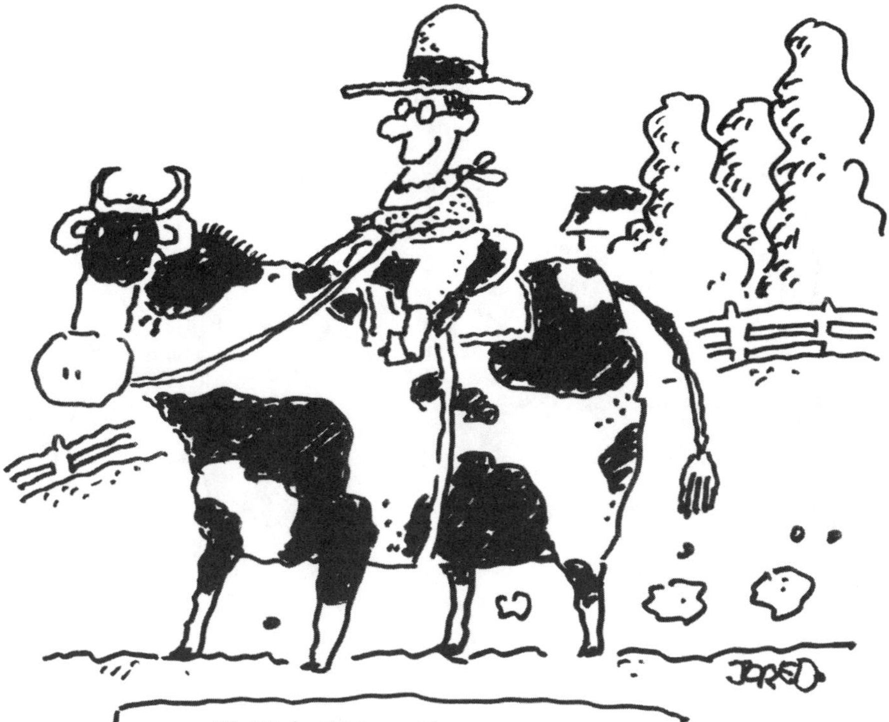
JARED

WENDELL THOUGHT COWBOYS RODE COWS.

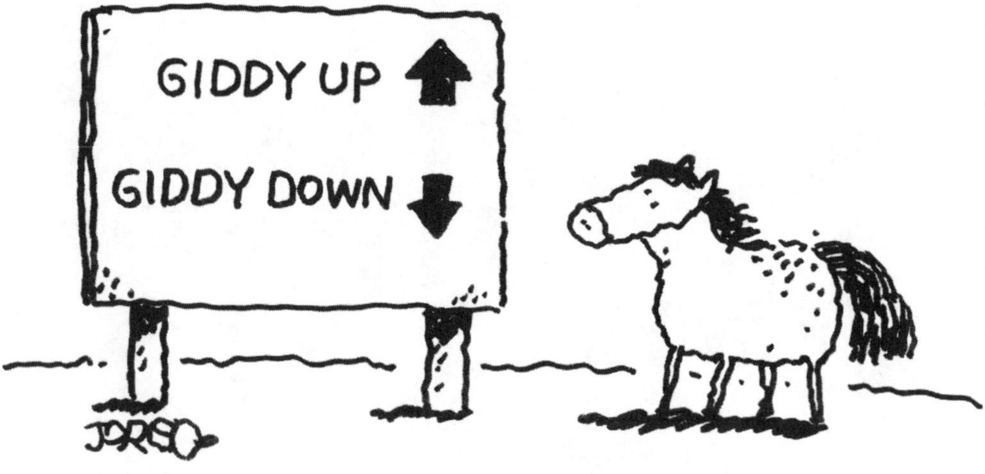
GIDDY UP
GIDDY DOWN
JORSO

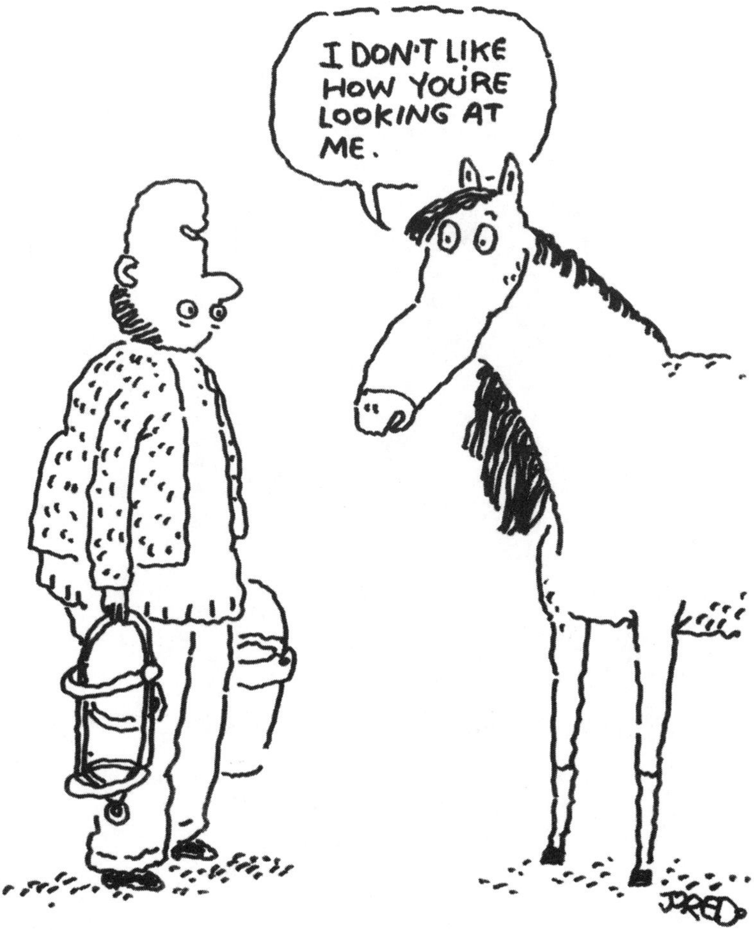
I DON'T LIKE HOW YOU'RE LOOKING AT ME.
JARED

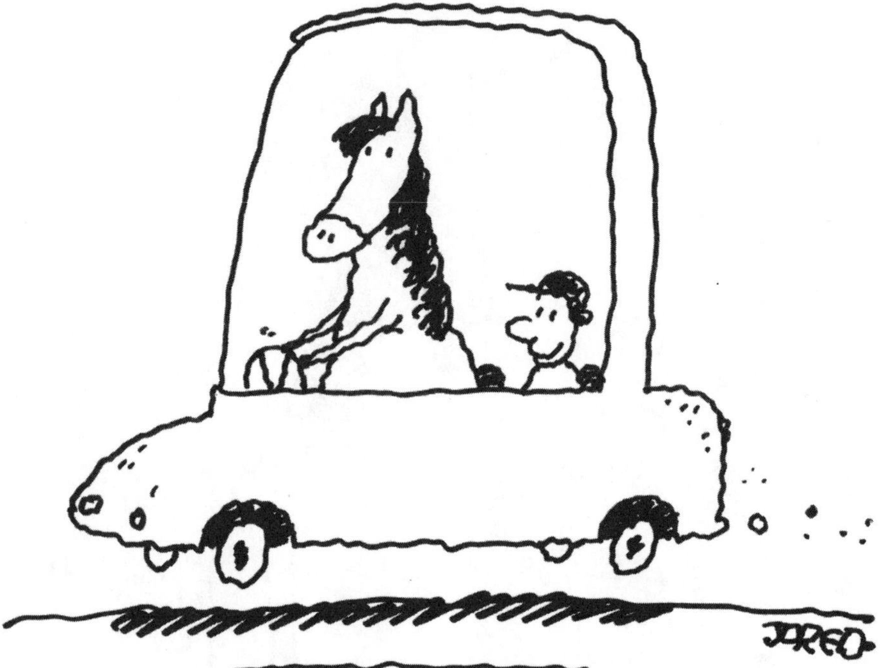
JARED

HORSE AND RIDER

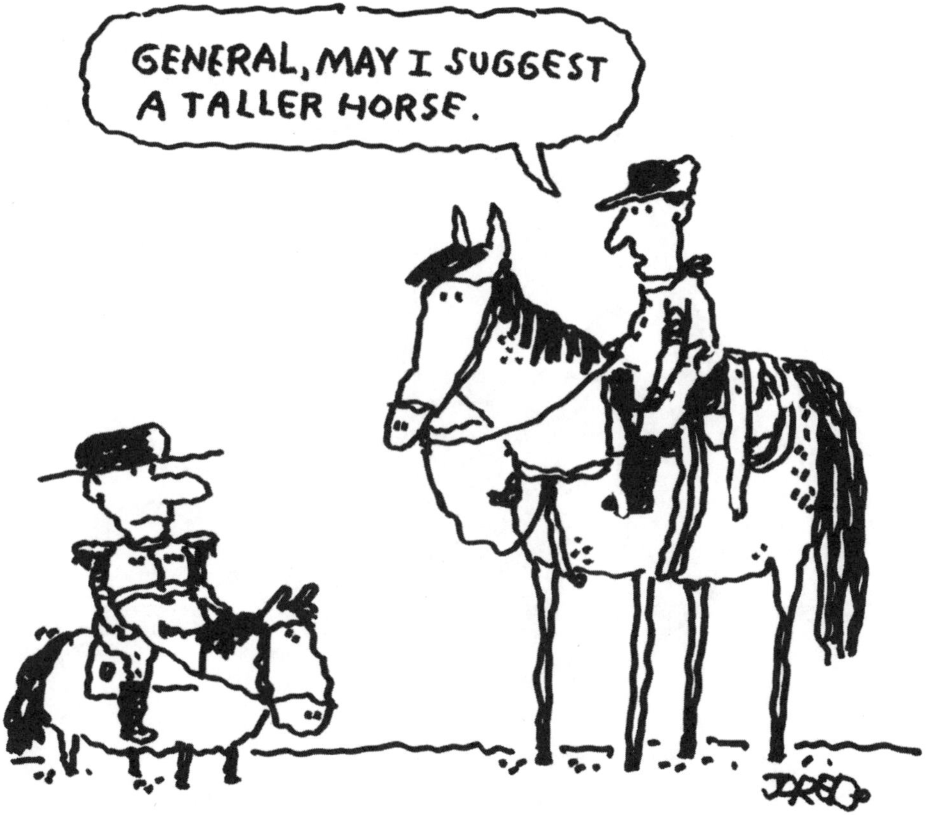
GENERAL, MAY I SUGGEST A TALLER HORSE.
JOREO

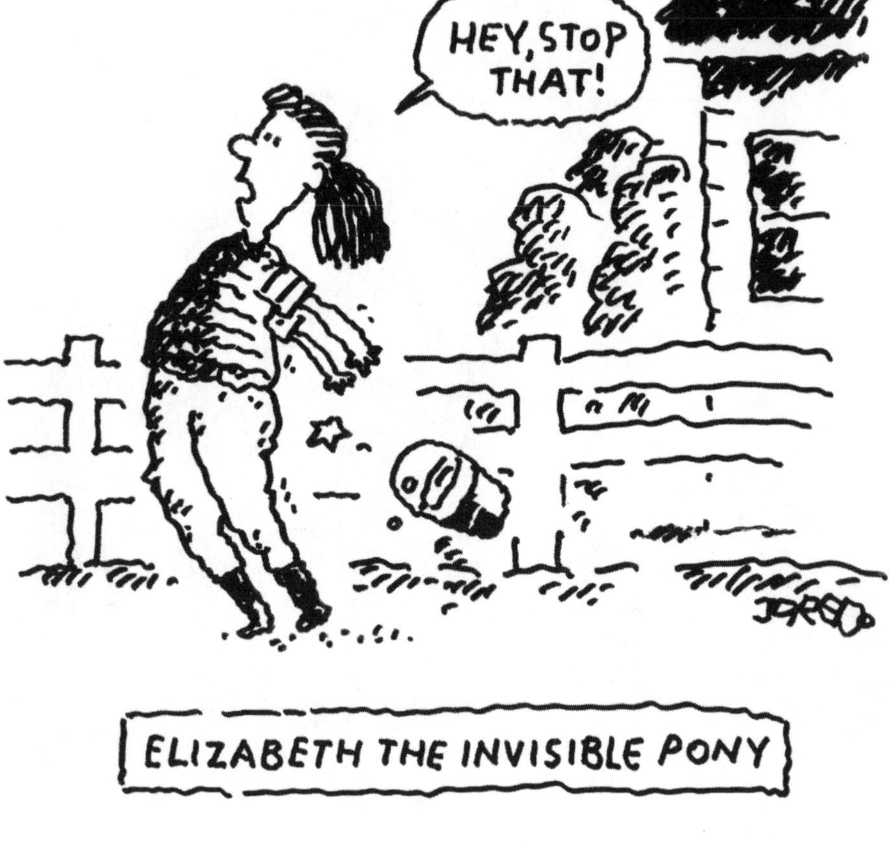
HEY, STOP THAT!

ELIZABETH THE INVISIBLE PONY

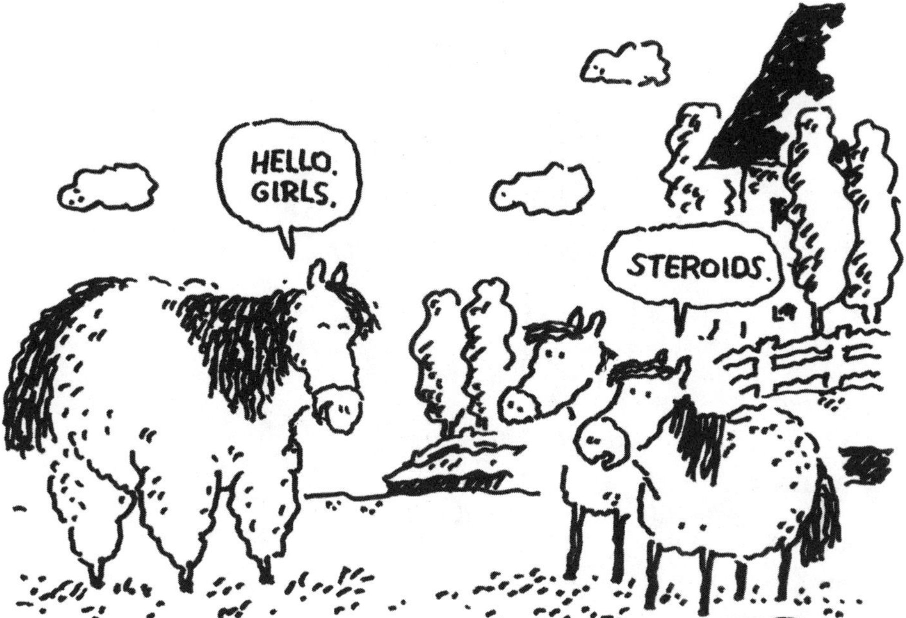
HELLO. GIRLS.
STEROIDS.

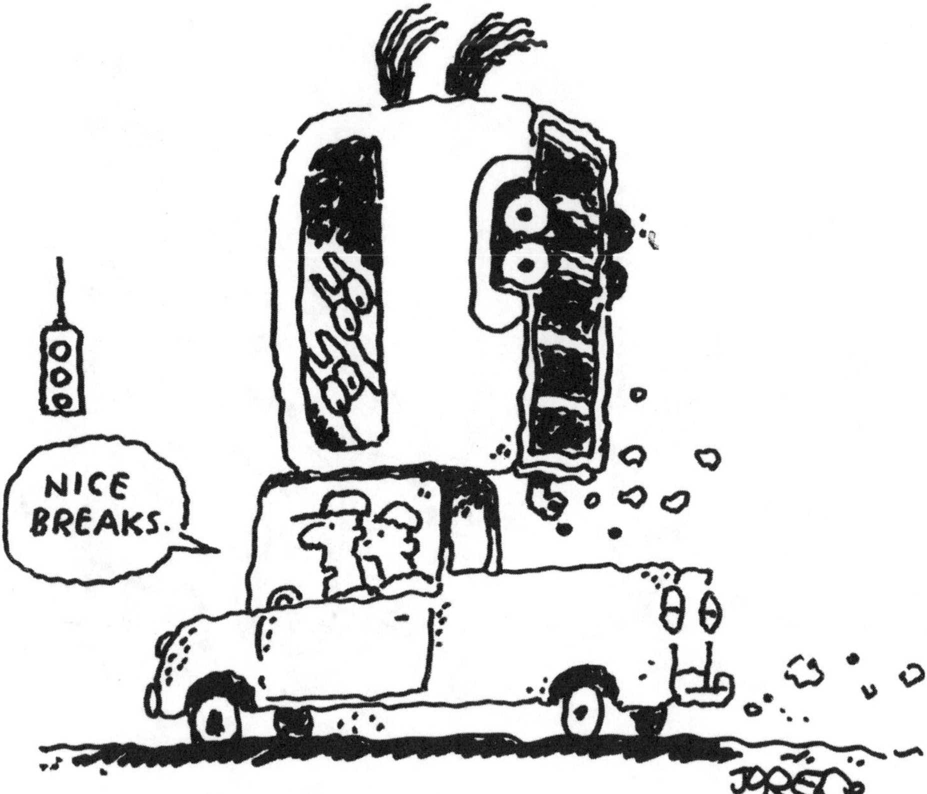
NICE BREAKS.
JORED

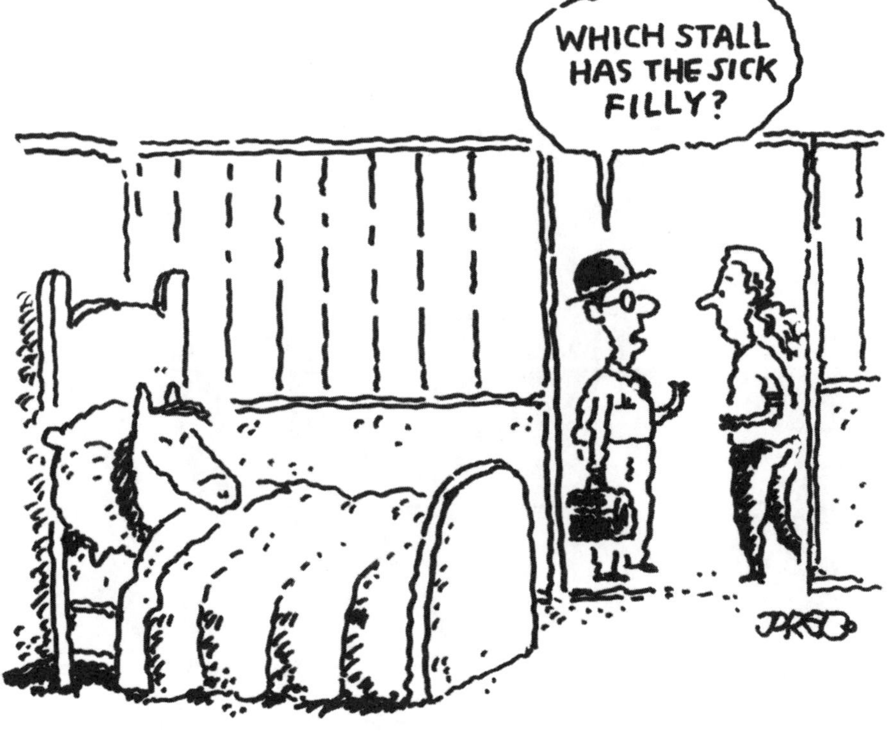
WHICH STALL HAS THE SICK FILLY?
JORGE

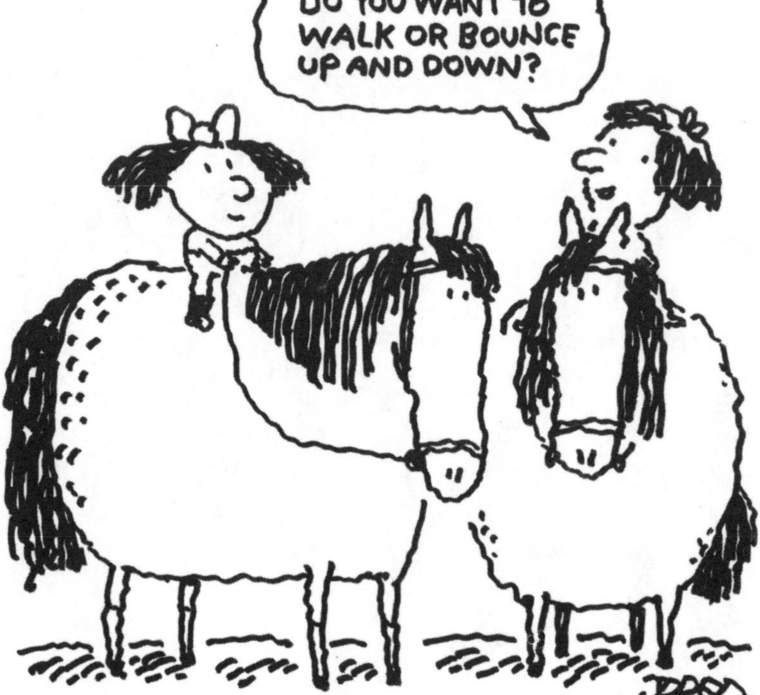
DO YOU WANT TO WALK OR BOUNCE UP AND DOWN?
JARED

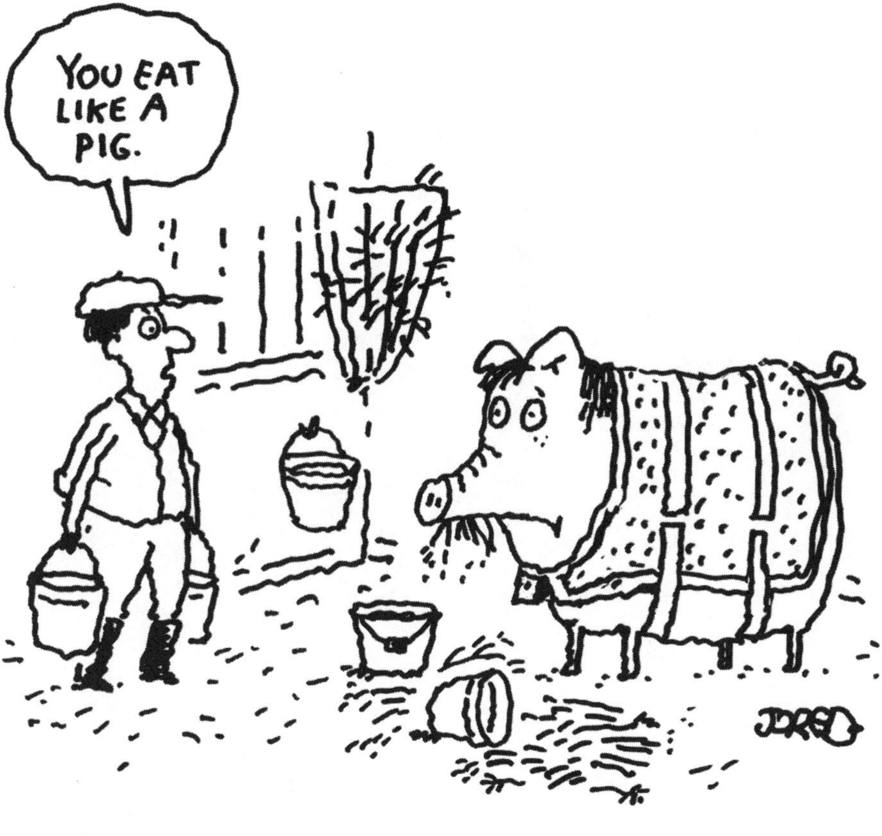
YOU EAT LIKE A PIG.
JORED

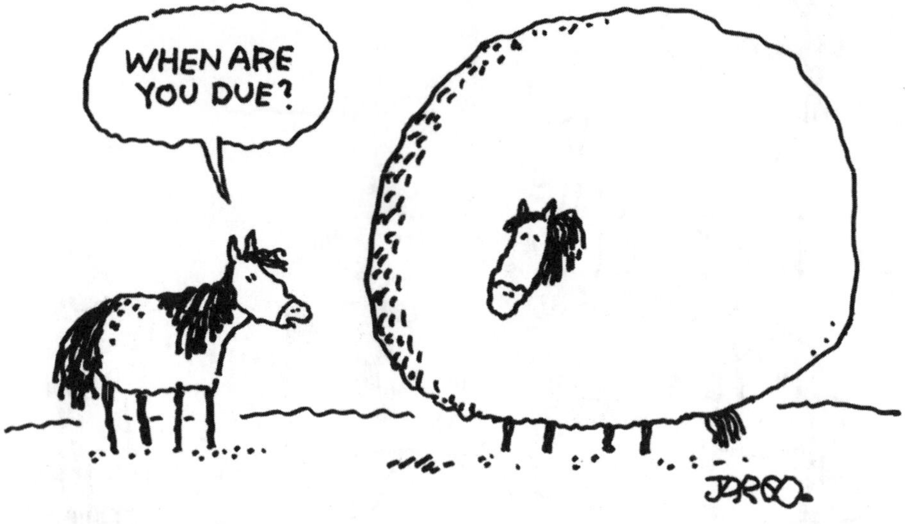
WHEN ARE YOU DUE?
JARGO

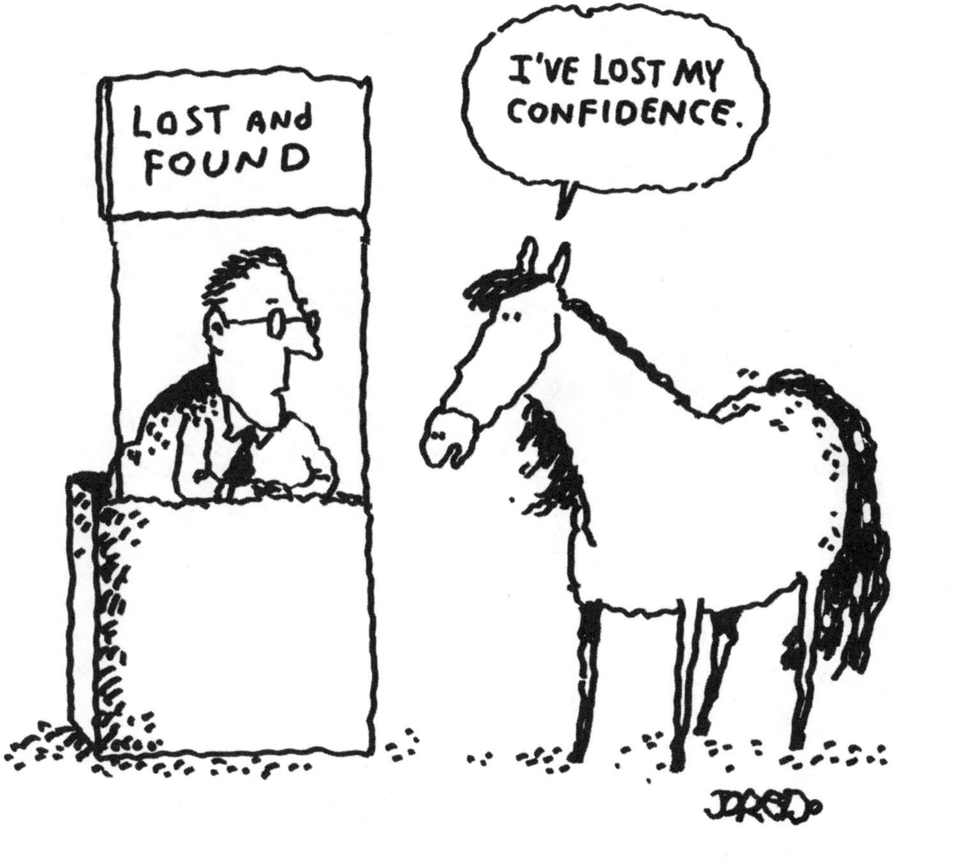
LOST AND FOUND
I'VE LOST MY CONFIDENCE.
JARED

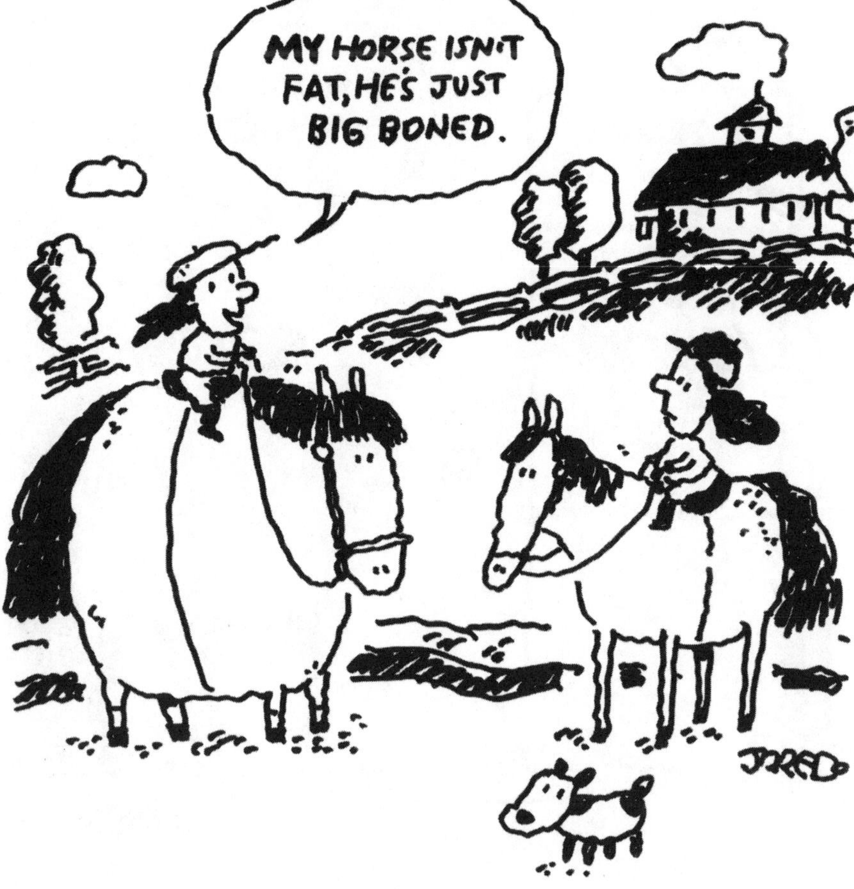
MY HORSE ISN'T FAT, HE'S JUST BIG BONED.
JARED

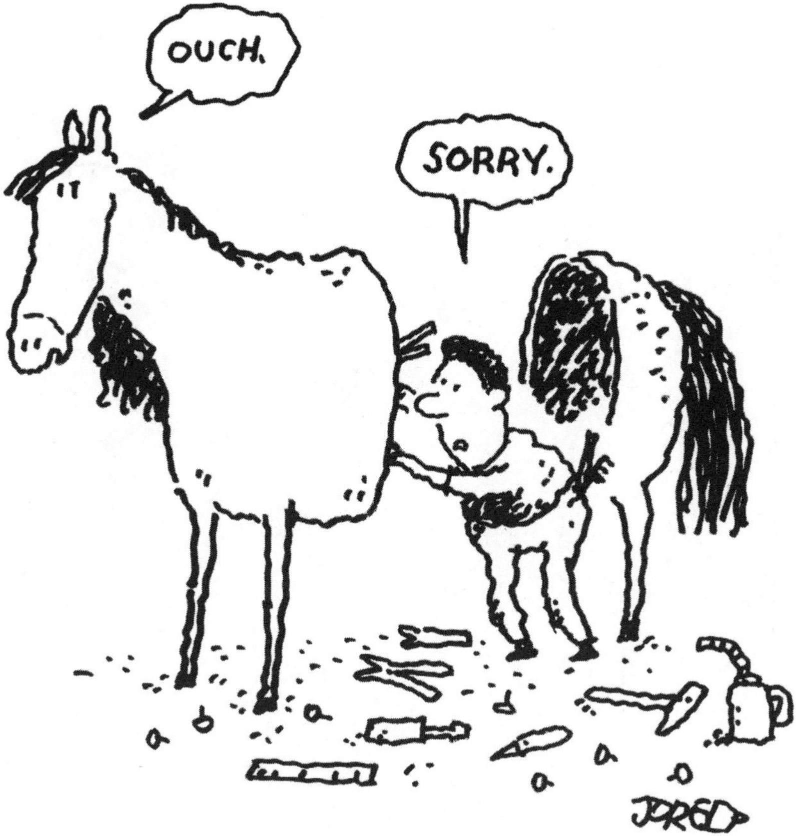
OUCH.
SORRY.
JARED

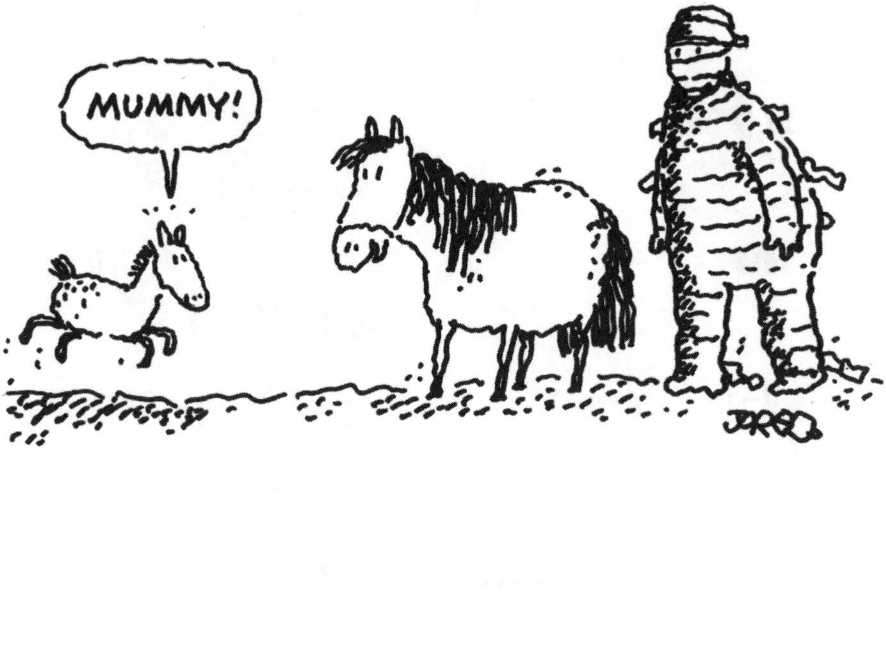
MUMMY!
JARED

TAILGATE PARTY

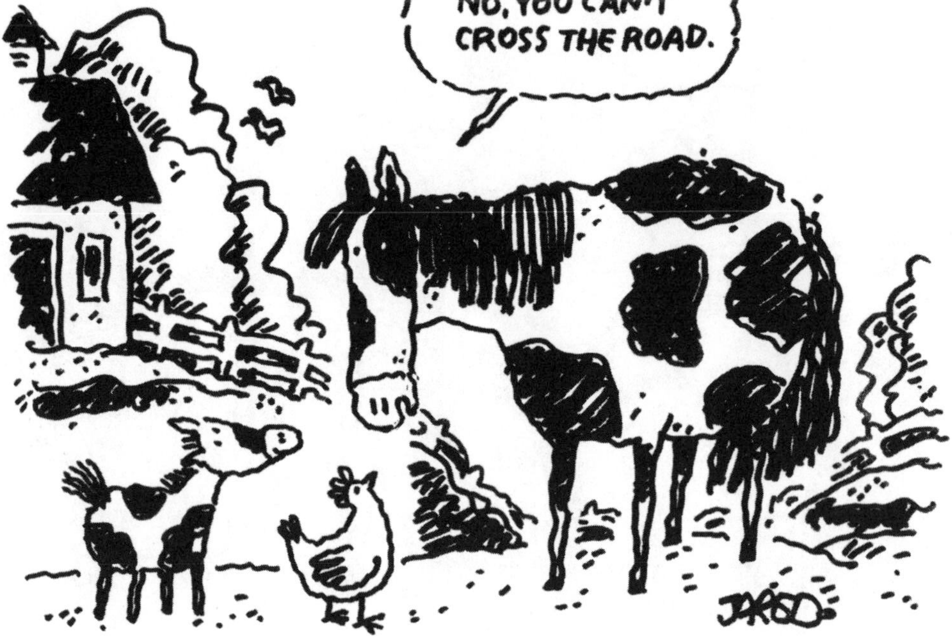
NO, YOU CAN'T CROSS THE ROAD.

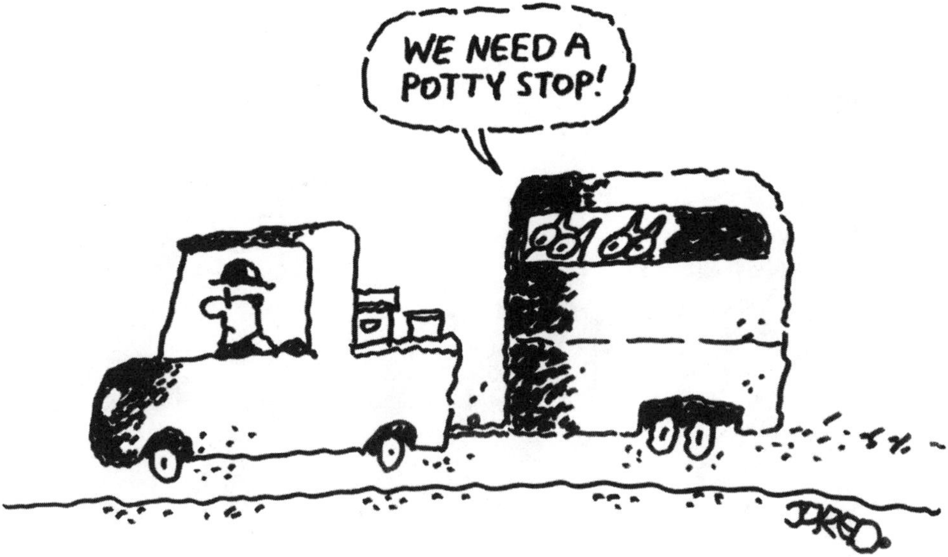
WE NEED A POTTY STOP!
JoREO

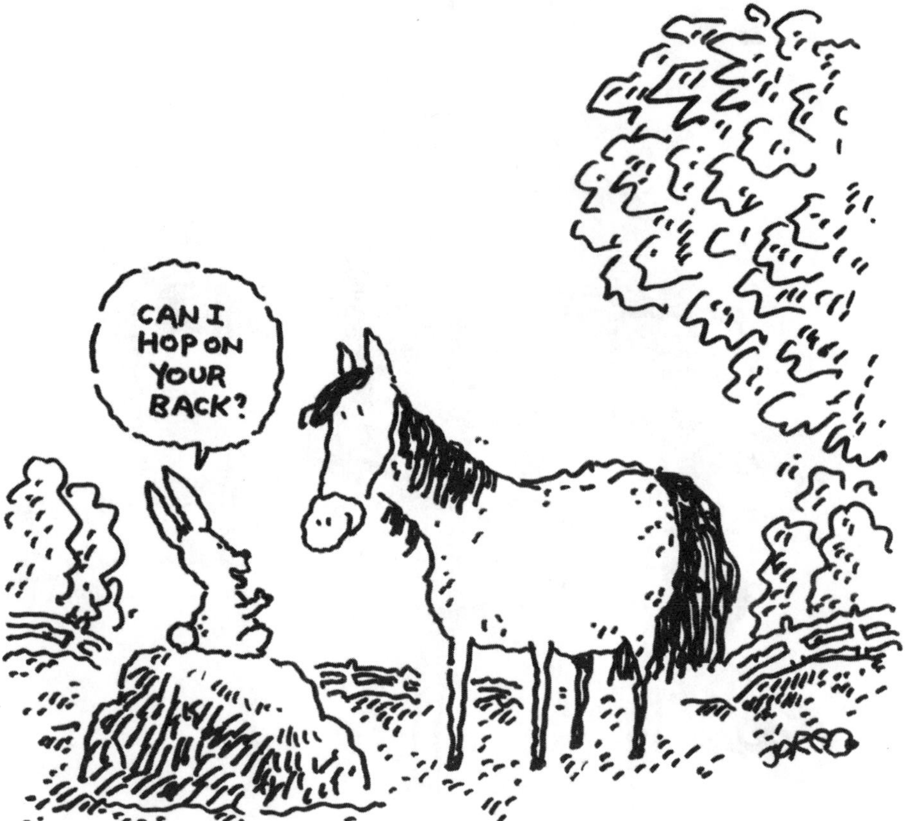
CAN I HOP ON YOUR BACK?
JORED

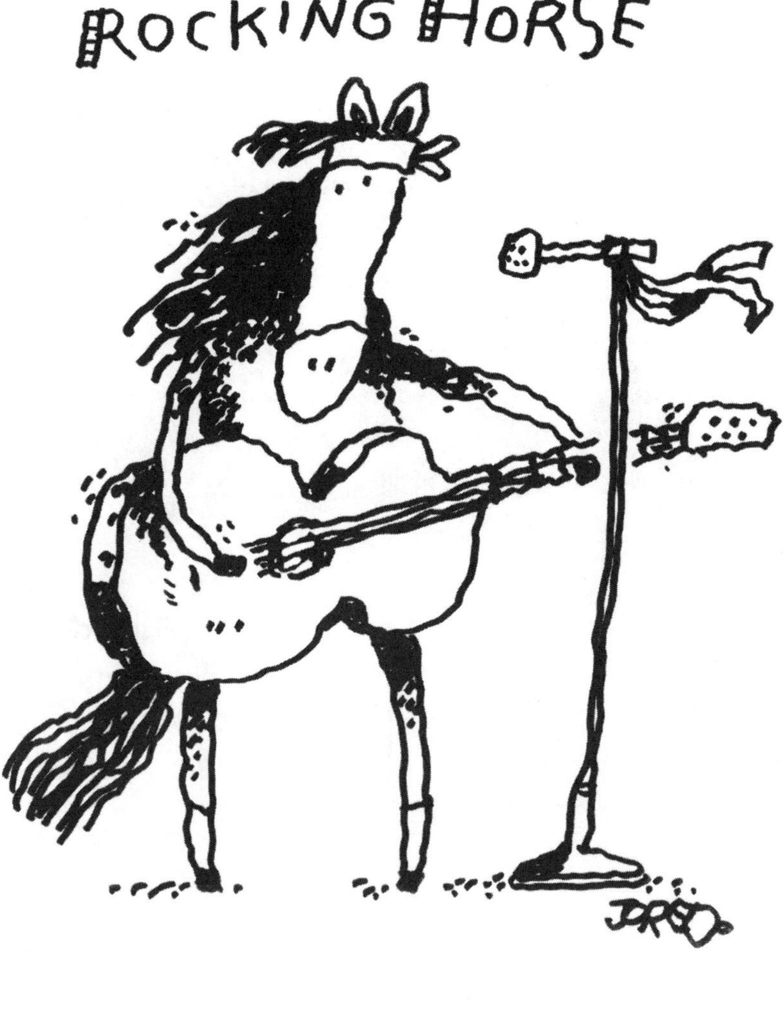
ROCKING HORSE

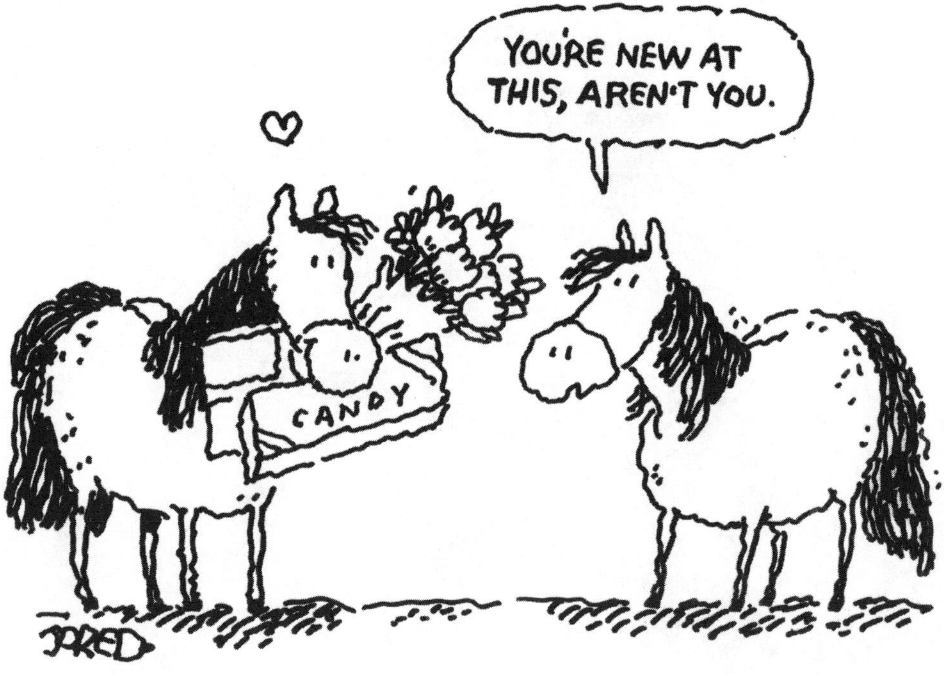

YOU'RE NEW AT THIS, AREN'T YOU.
CANDY
JARED

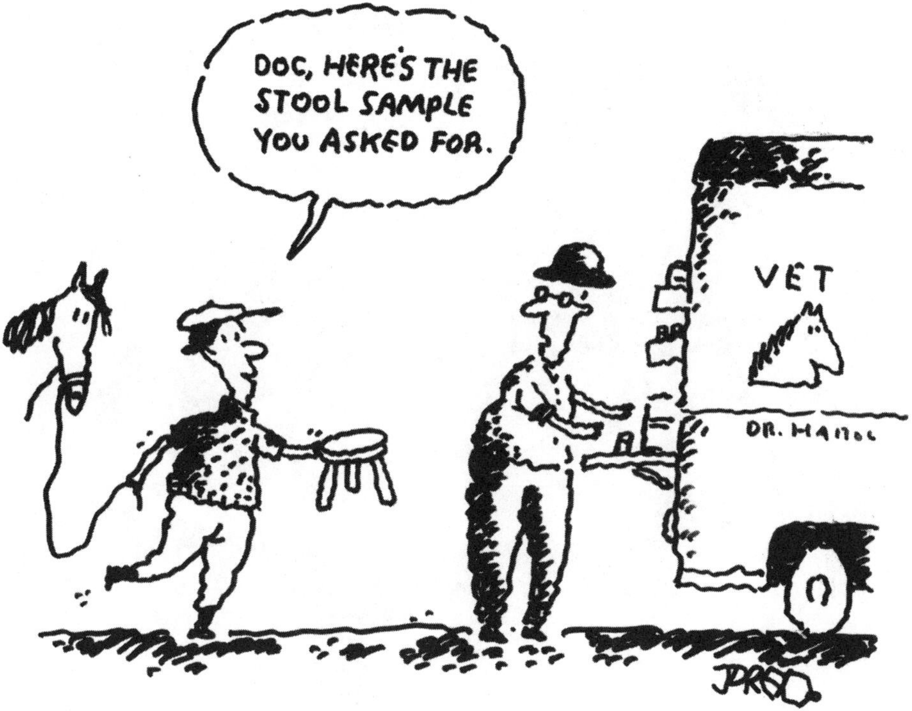
DOC, HERE'S THE STOOL SAMPLE YOU ASKED FOR.
VET

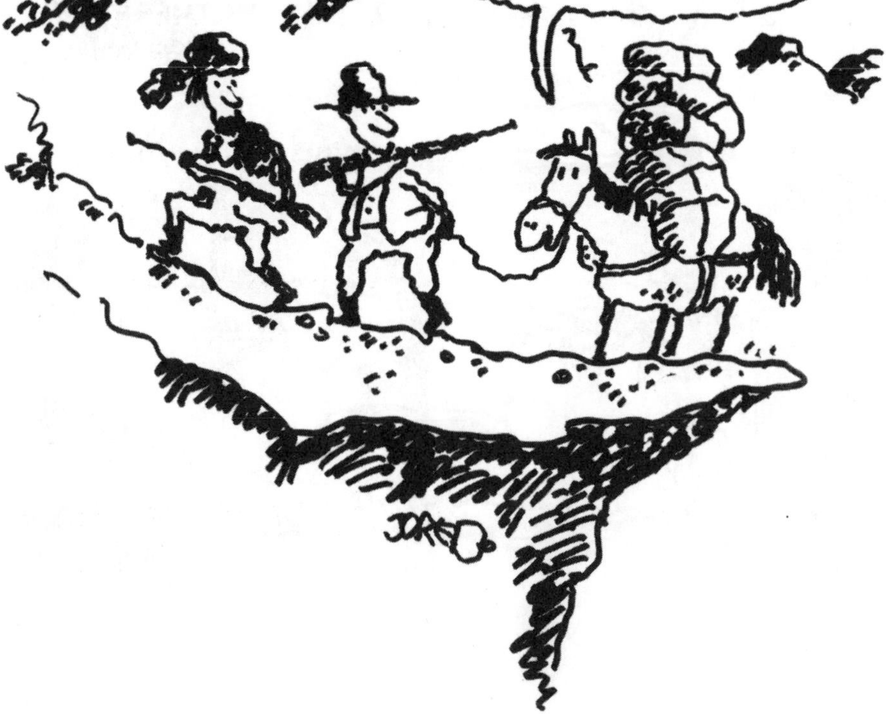
GEE GUYS, THIS HAS BEEN A WONDERFUL TRIP, BUT I THINK I'LL CALL IT A DAY.
JORED

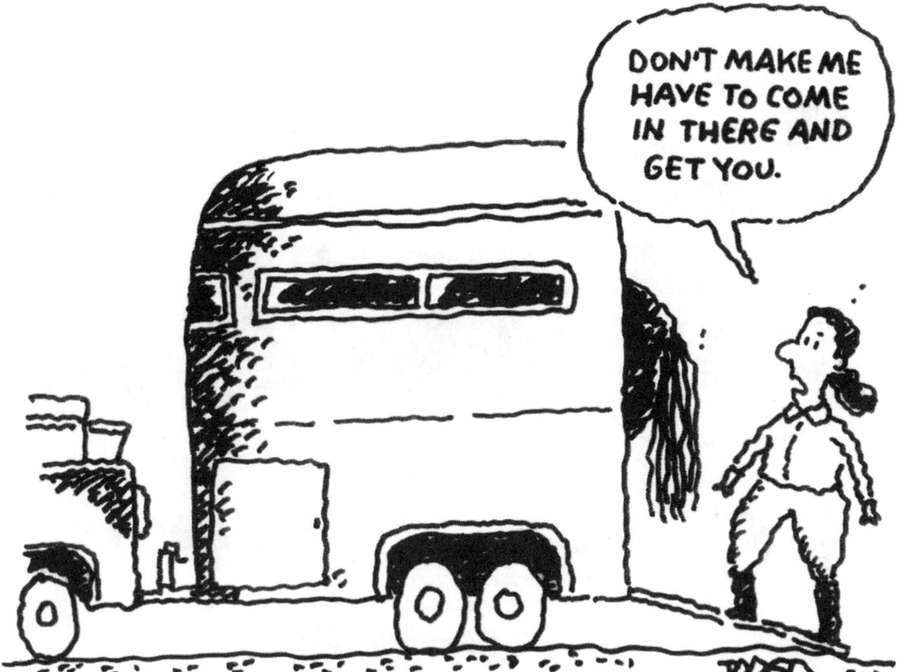
DON'T MAKE ME HAVE TO COME IN THERE AND GET YOU.
JARED

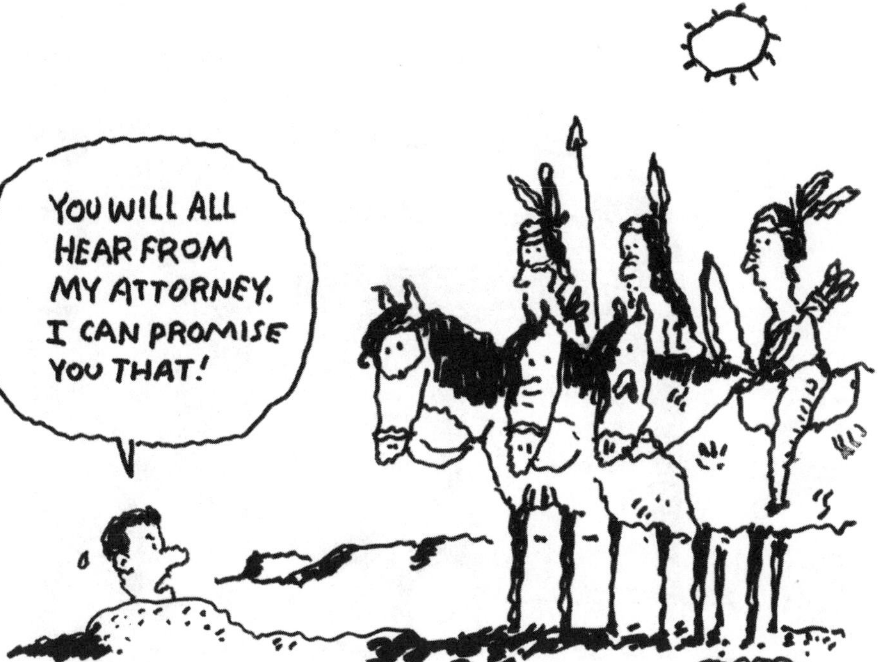
YOU WILL ALL HEAR FROM MY ATTORNEY. I CAN PROMISE YOU THAT!
JARED

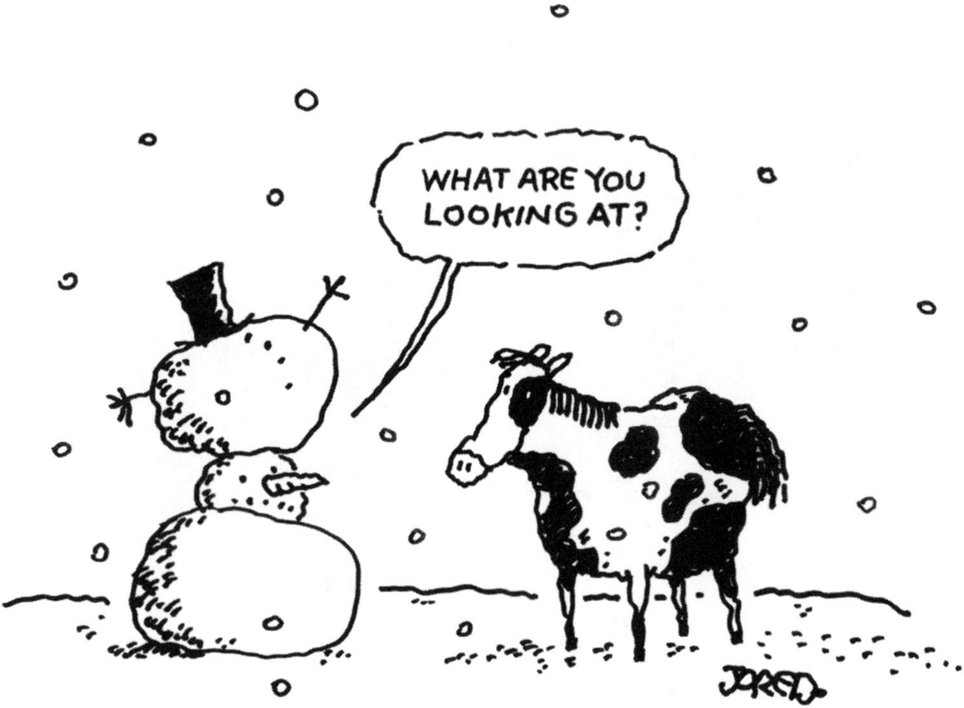
WHAT ARE YOU LOOKING AT?
JARED

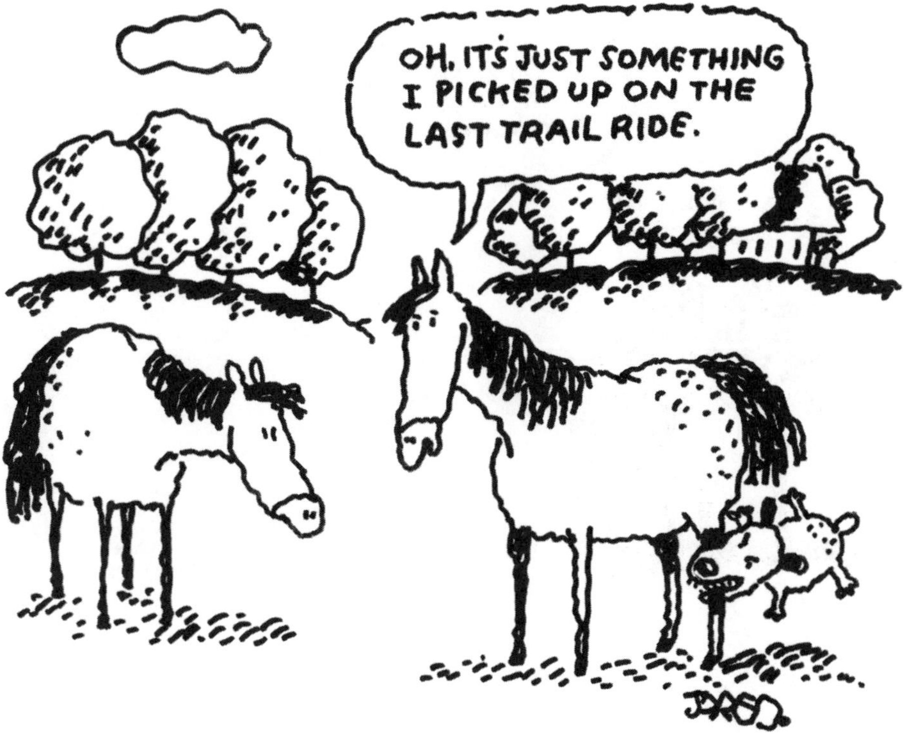
OH, IT'S JUST SOMETHING I PICKED UP ON THE LAST TRAIL RIDE.
JARED

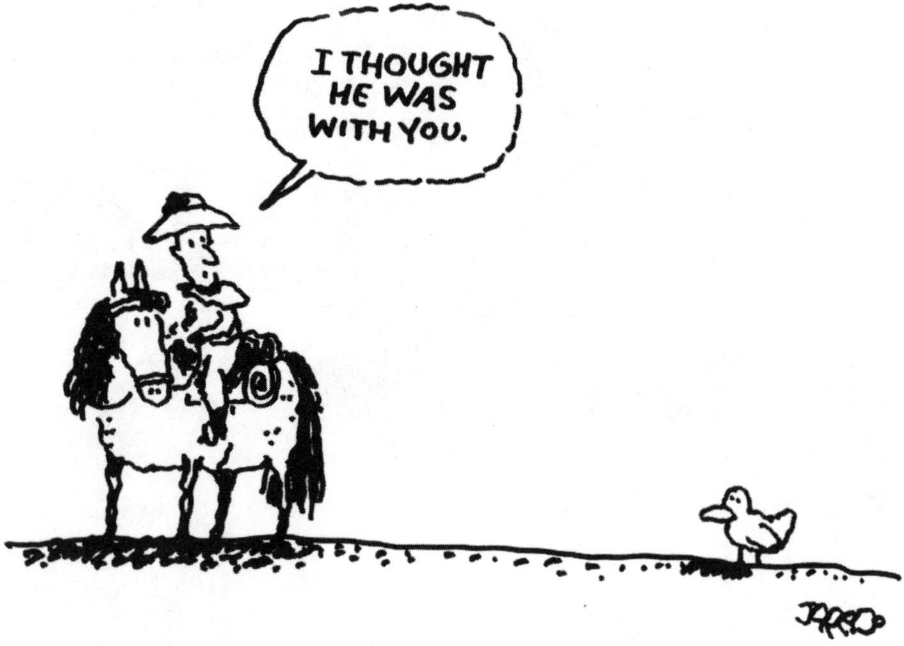
I THOUGHT HE WAS WITH YOU.
JARROP

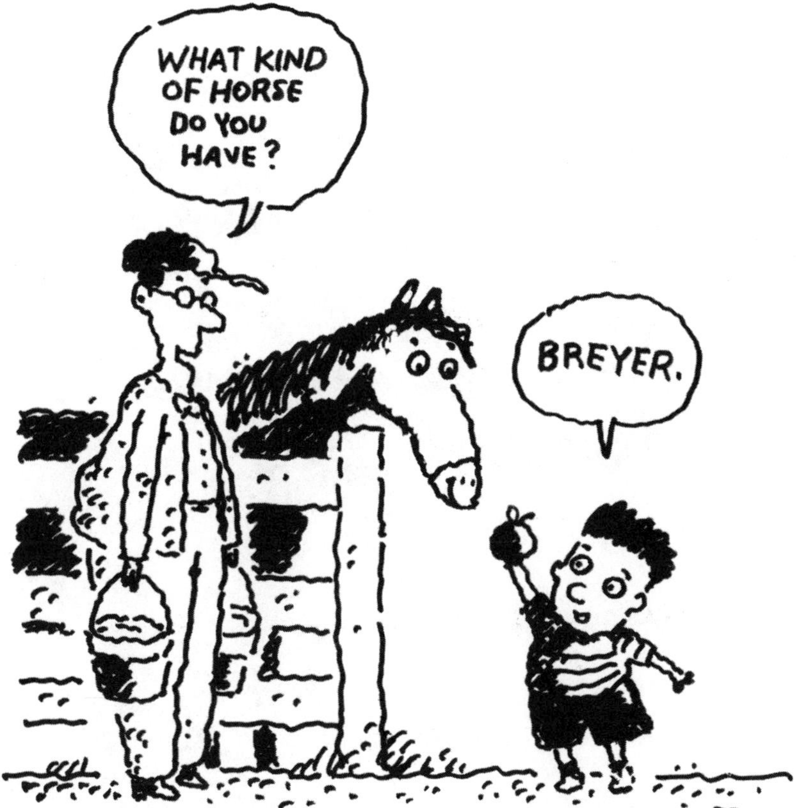
WHAT KIND OF HORSE DO YOU HAVE?
BREYER.
JORED

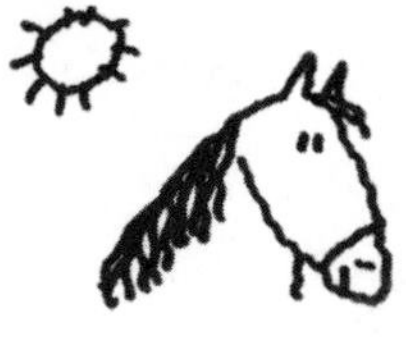

THE "PERFECT" HORSE SHOW

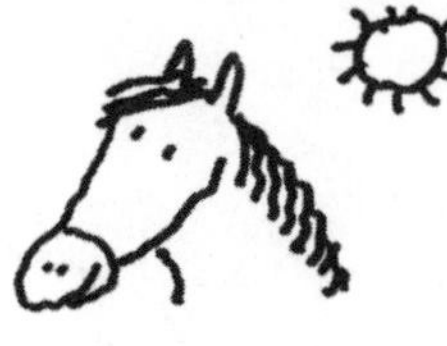

1. NO ENTRY OR SHOW FEES.

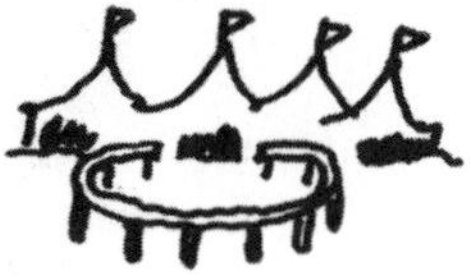

2. ALL HORSES WILL BE STALLED NEAR THE SHOW RING.

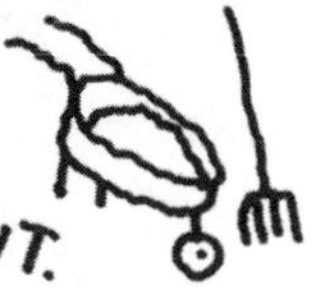

3. STALLS WILL BE CLEANED OUT DAILY BY SHOW MANAGEMENT.

4. NO JUDGES.

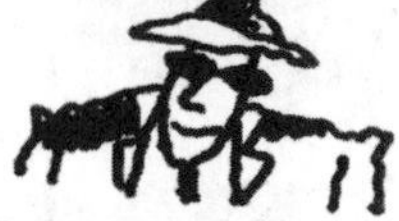

5. EACH EXHIBITOR WILL:

   (A) MARK THEIR OWN JUDGE'S CARD.

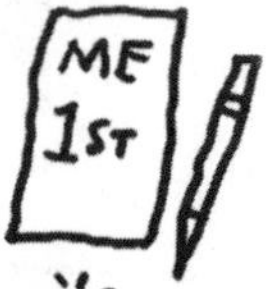
ME
1ST

   (B) RECEIVE A TROPHY, BLUE RIBBON AND CASH MONEY.

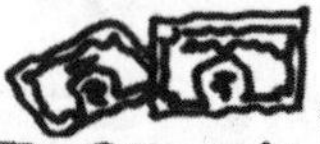

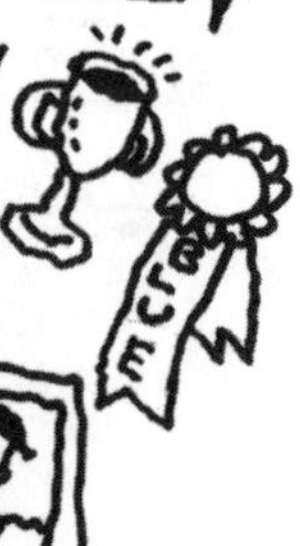

   (C) RECEIVE A COLORED PHOTOGRAPH OF THEIR "VICTORY PASS."

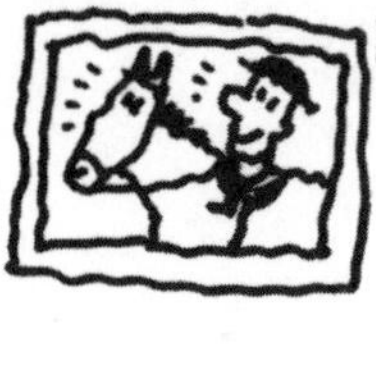

6. EVERYONE'S DAUGHTER IS CROWNED "SHOW QUEEN."

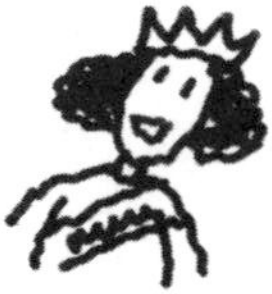

7. EXHIBITORS WILL "SINCERELY" CONGRATULATE EACH OTHER AT THE GALA BANQUET AND DANCE.

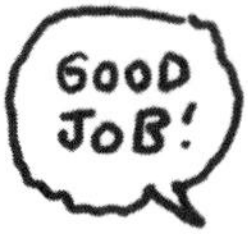
GOOD JOB!

8. TRAILERS WILL BE UNLOADED AND LOADED BY COMPLETE STRANGERS WHILE EXHIBITORS ARE SERVED CHILLED WINES AND IMPORTED CHEESE IN THE COOL HOSPITALITY TENT. (NO TIPPING PLEASE)

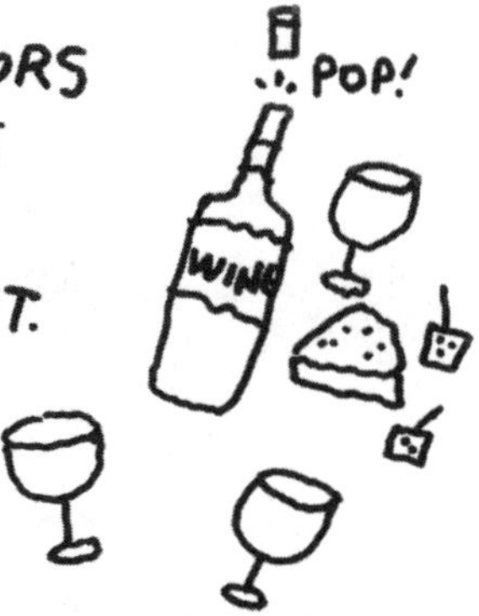
POP!
WINE

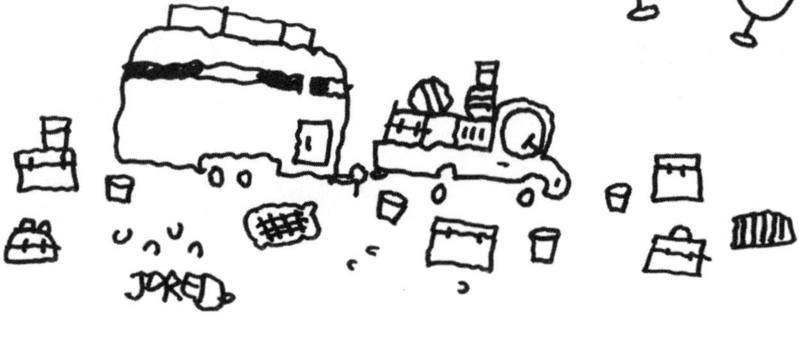

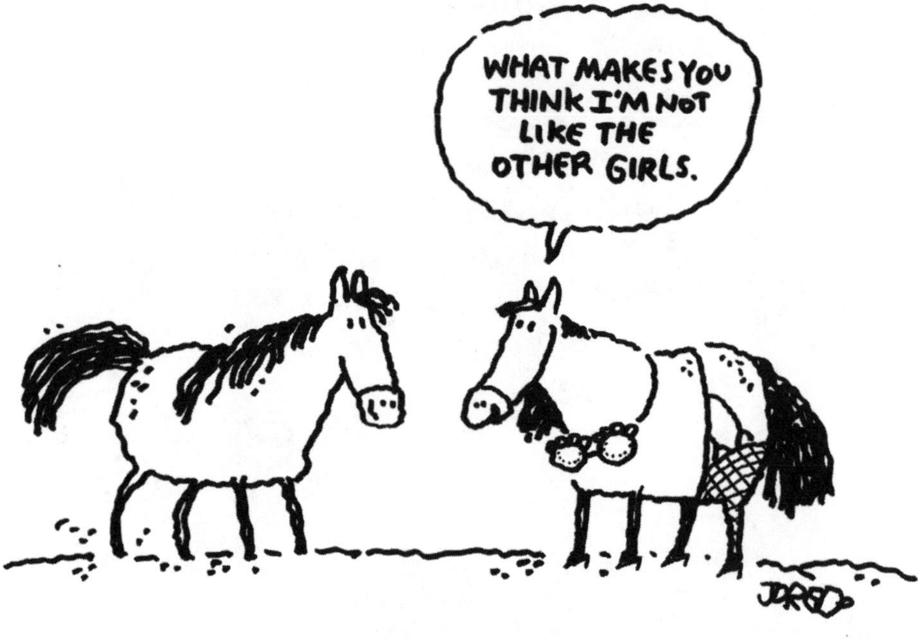
WHAT MAKES YOU THINK I'M NOT LIKE THE OTHER GIRLS.
JARED

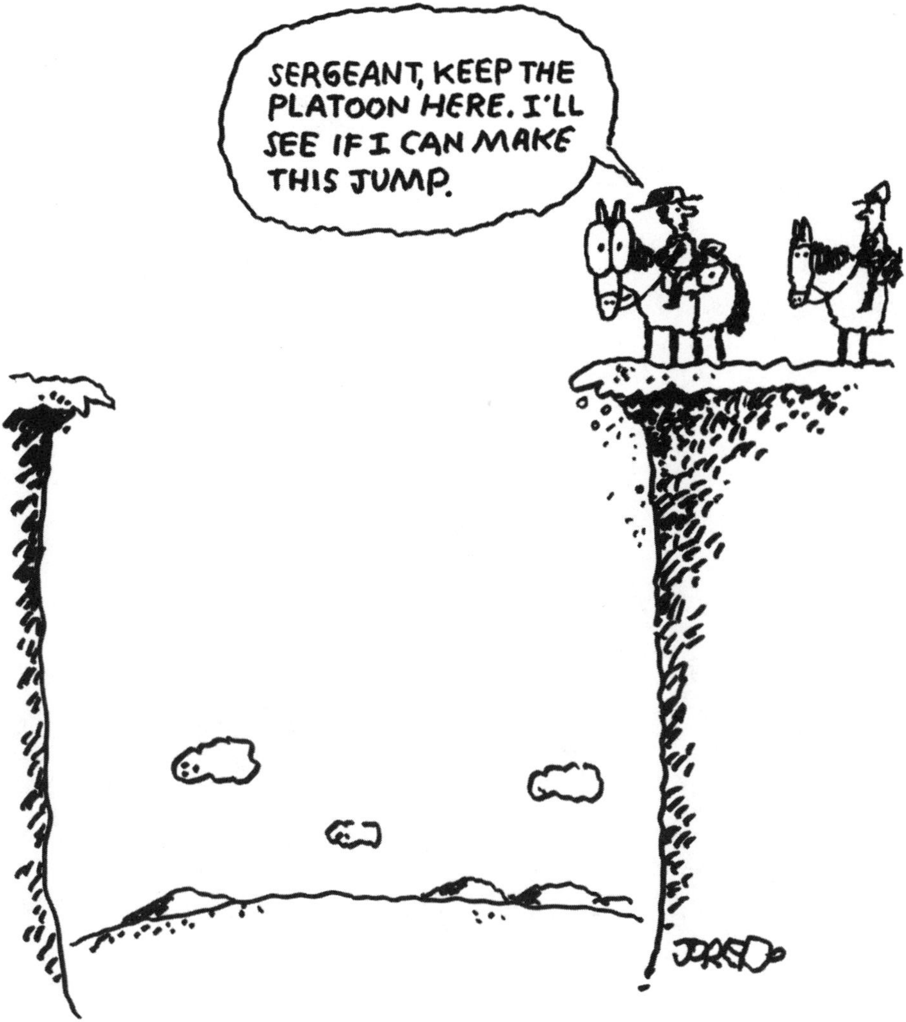
SERGEANT, KEEP THE PLATOON HERE. I'LL SEE IF I CAN MAKE THIS JUMP.

CARRY OUT SERVICE

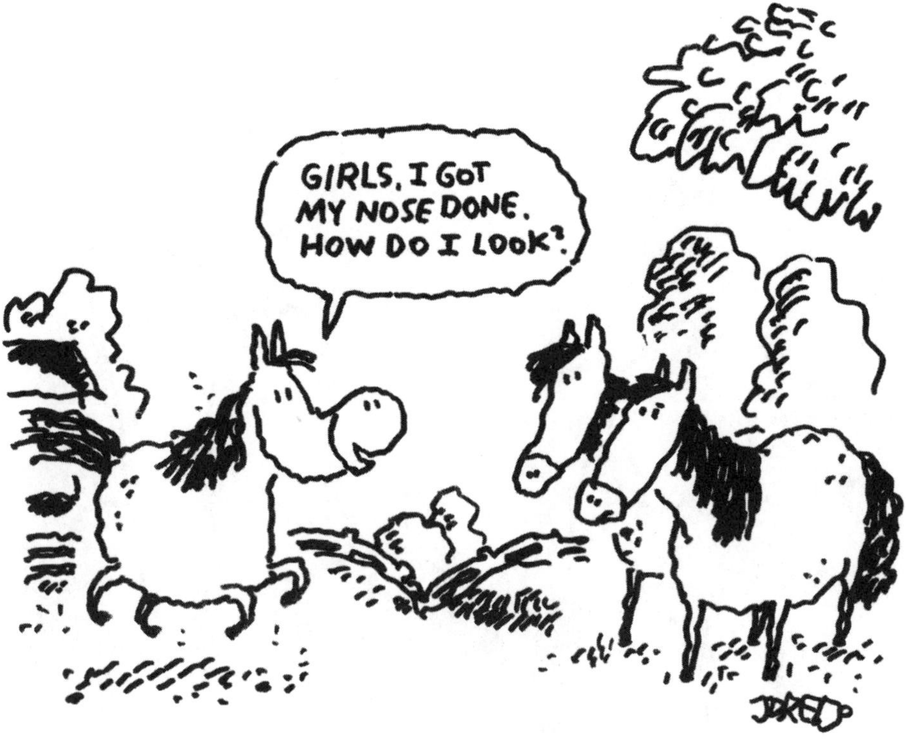
GIRLS, I GOT MY NOSE DONE. HOW DO I LOOK?
JARED

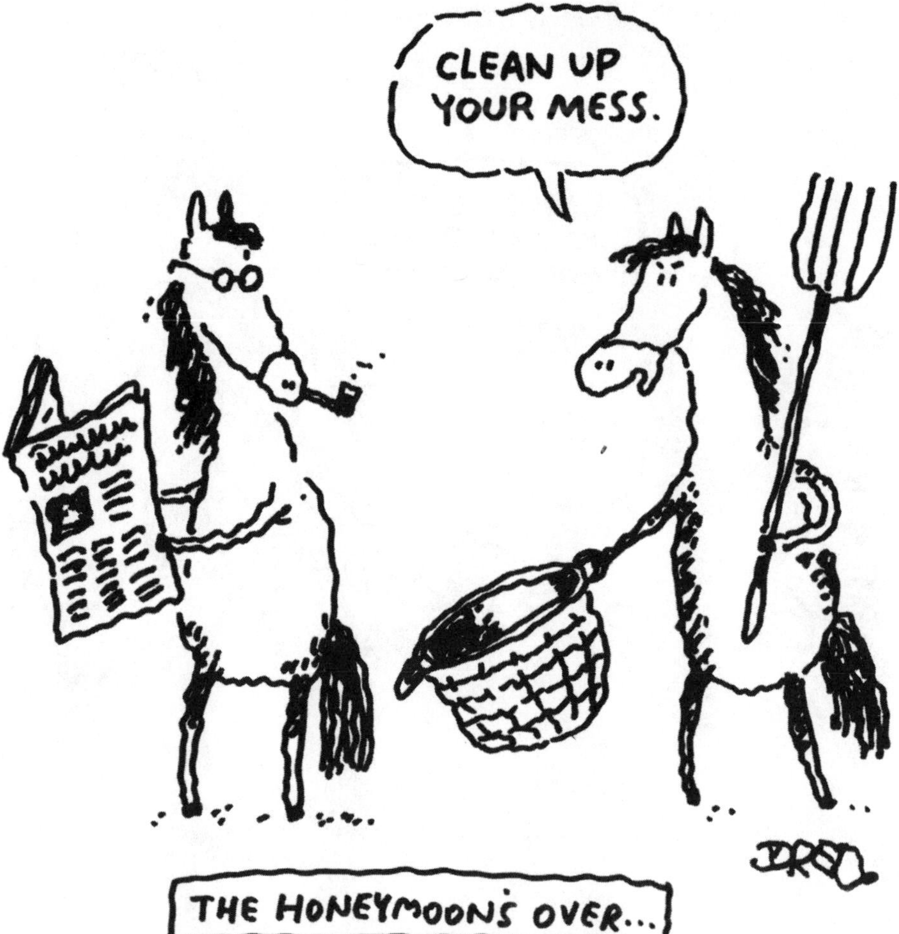
CLEAN UP YOUR MESS.

THE HONEYMOON'S OVER...

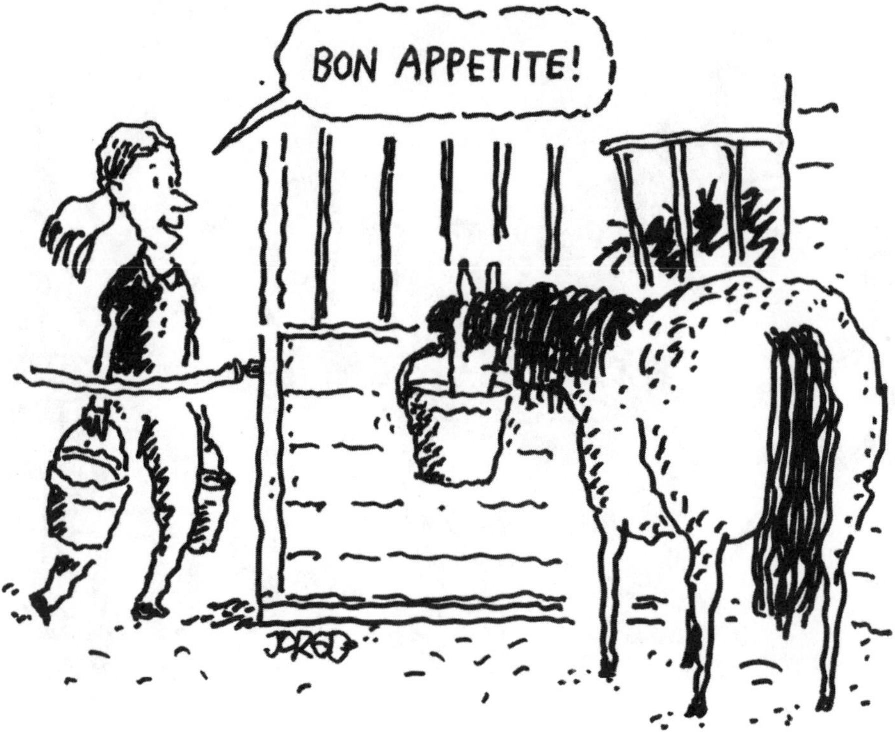
BON APPETITE!

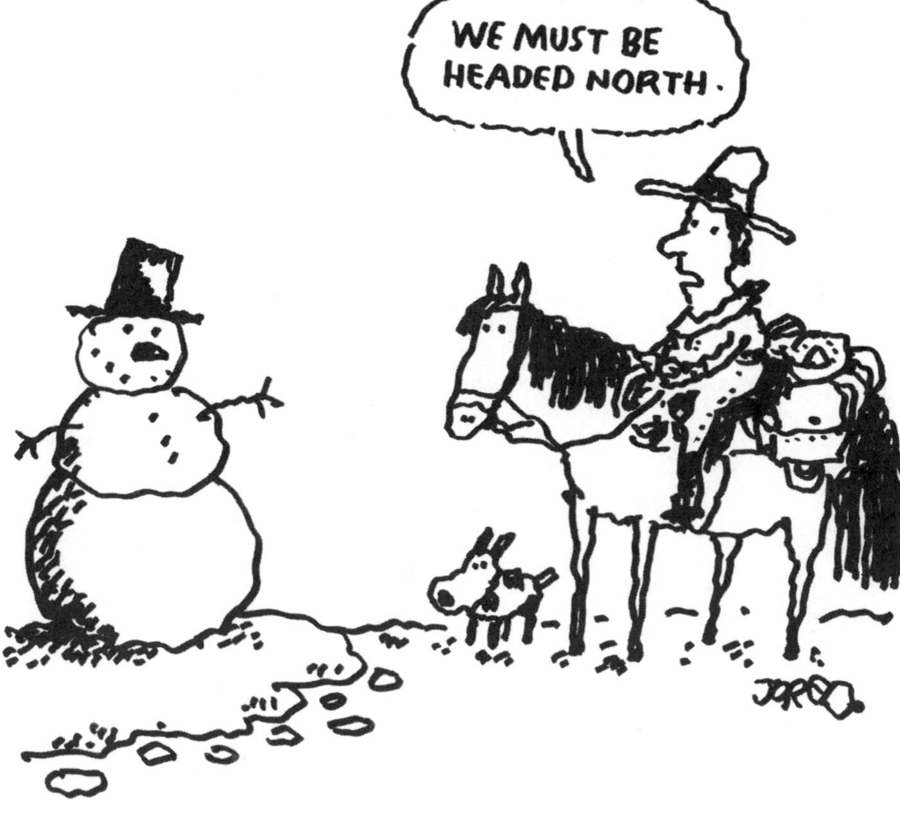
WE MUST BE HEADED NORTH.
JORSO

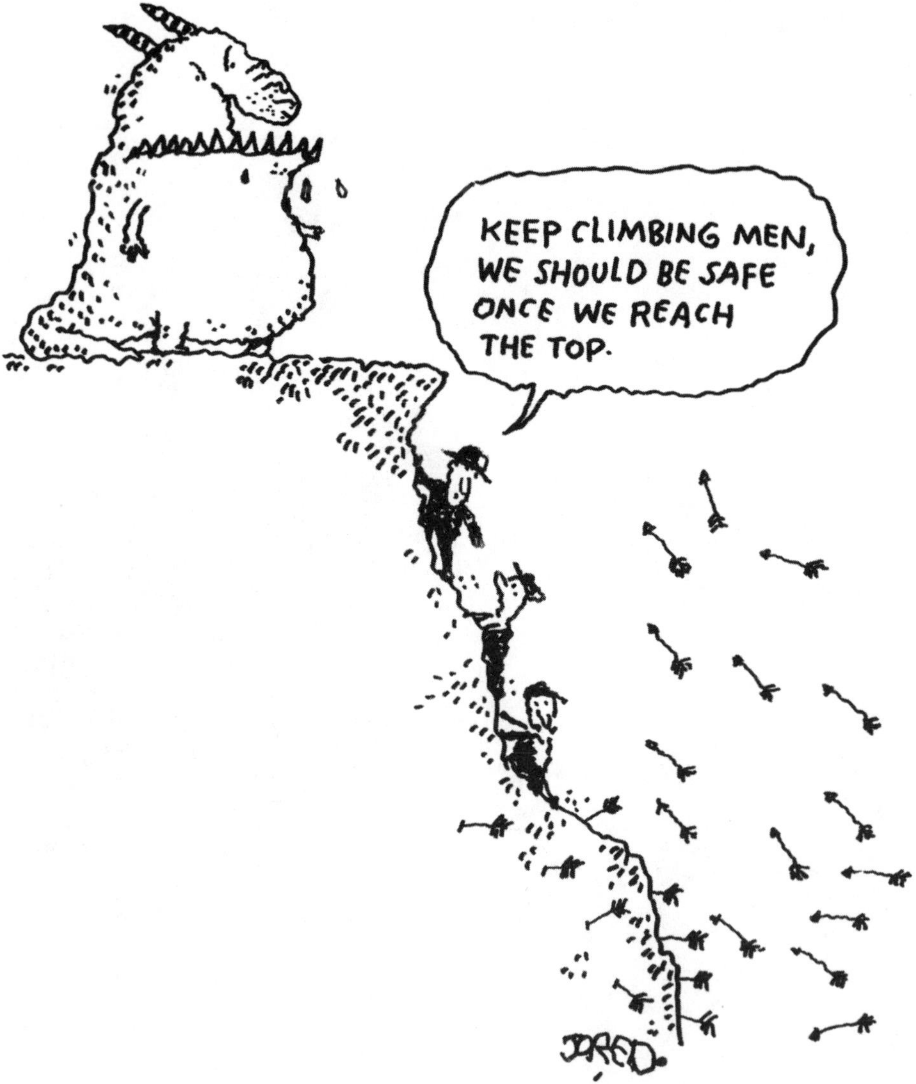
KEEP CLIMBING MEN, WE SHOULD BE SAFE ONCE WE REACH THE TOP.
JARED

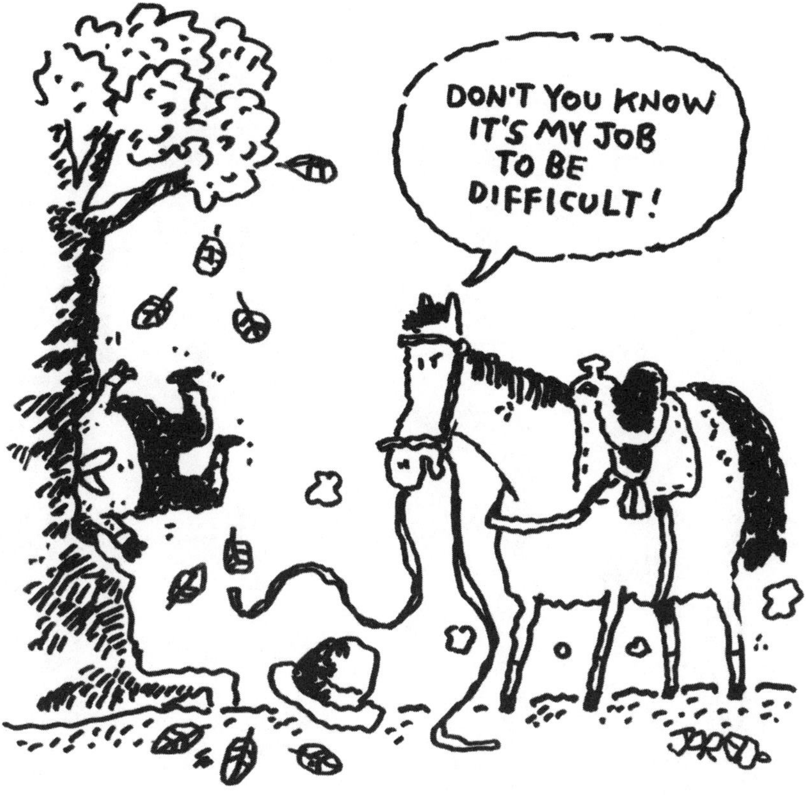
DON'T YOU KNOW IT'S MY JOB TO BE DIFFICULT!
JARED

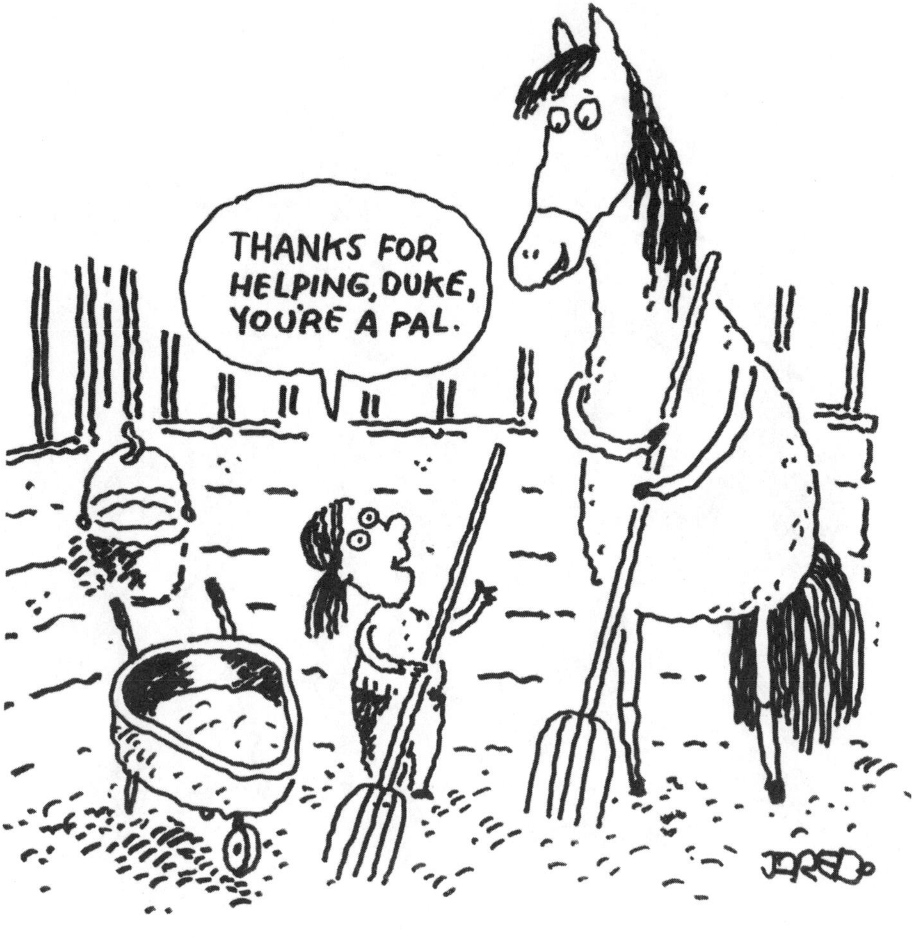
THANKS FOR HELPING, DUKE, YOU'RE A PAL.

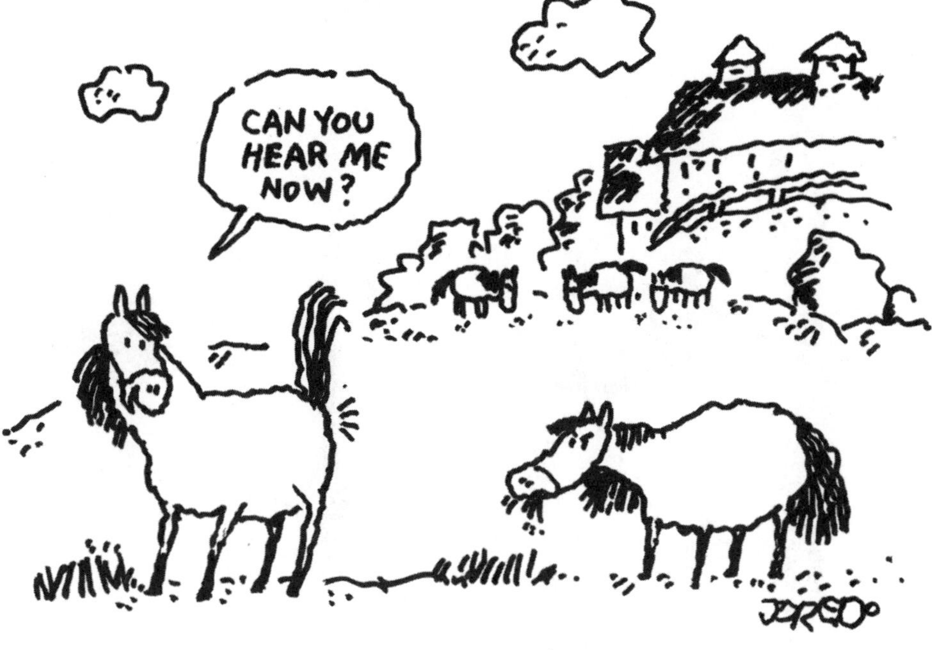
CAN YOU HEAR ME NOW?

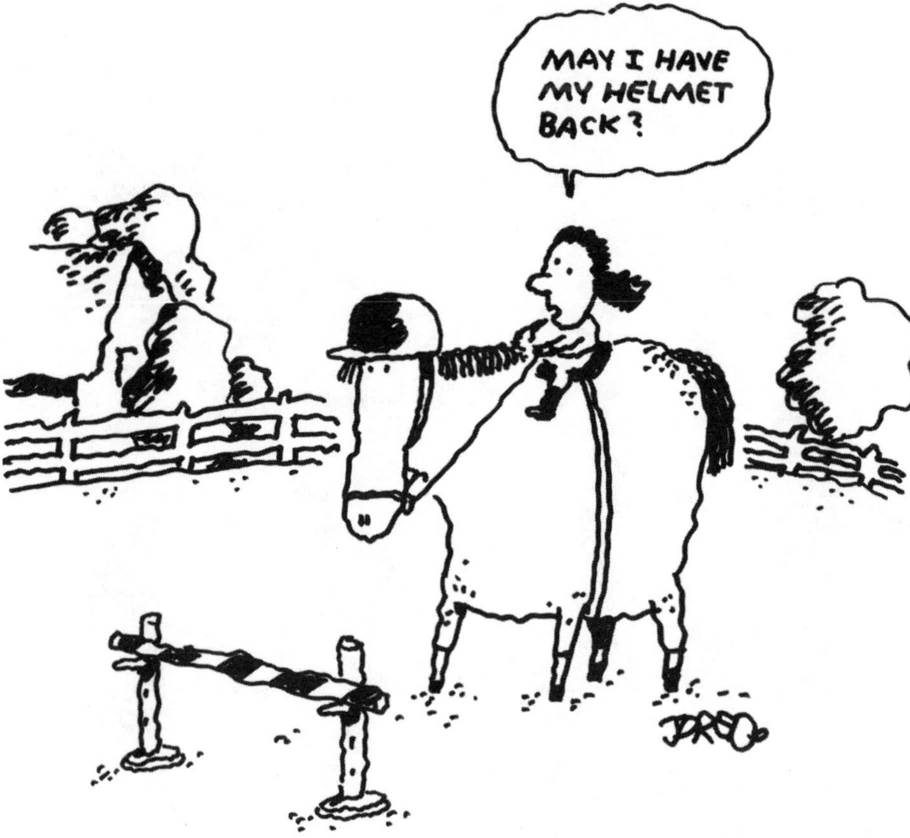
MAY I HAVE
MY HELMET
BACK?
JDREO

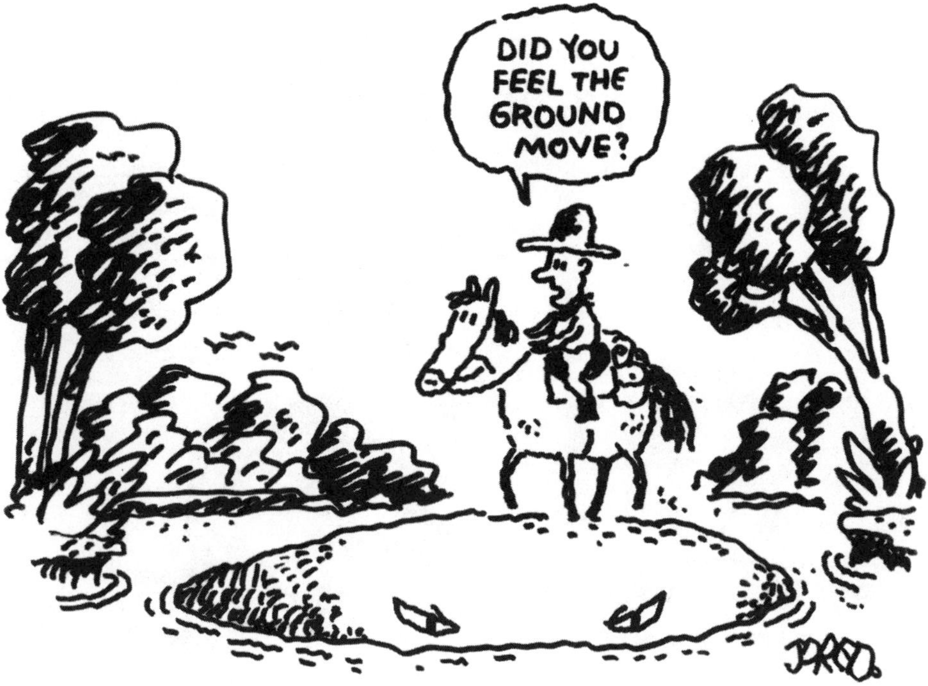
DID YOU FEEL THE GROUND MOVE?

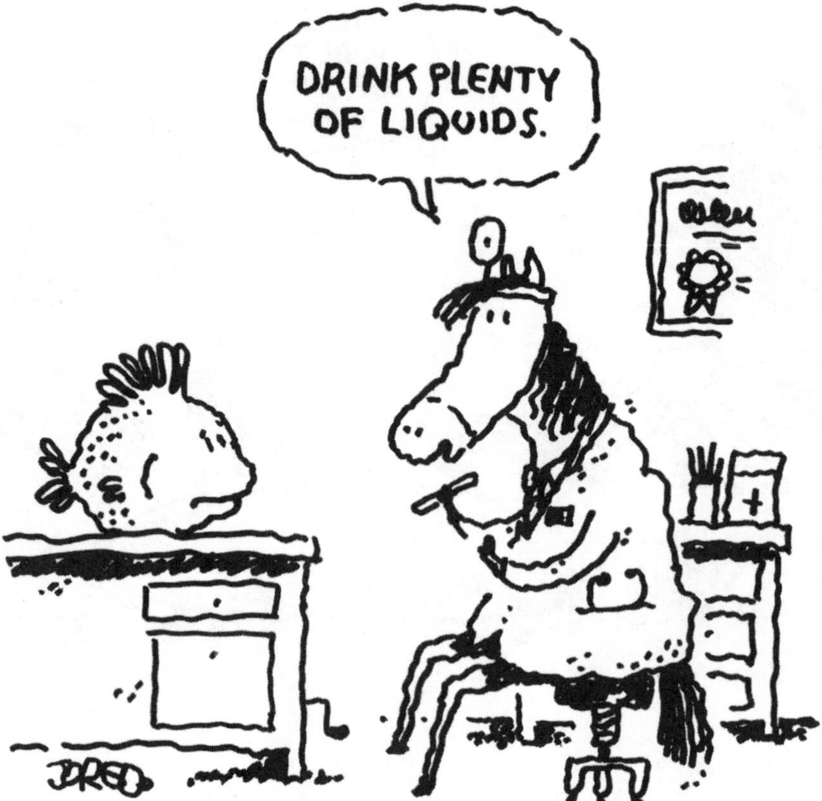
DRINK PLENTY OF LIQUIDS.
DREO

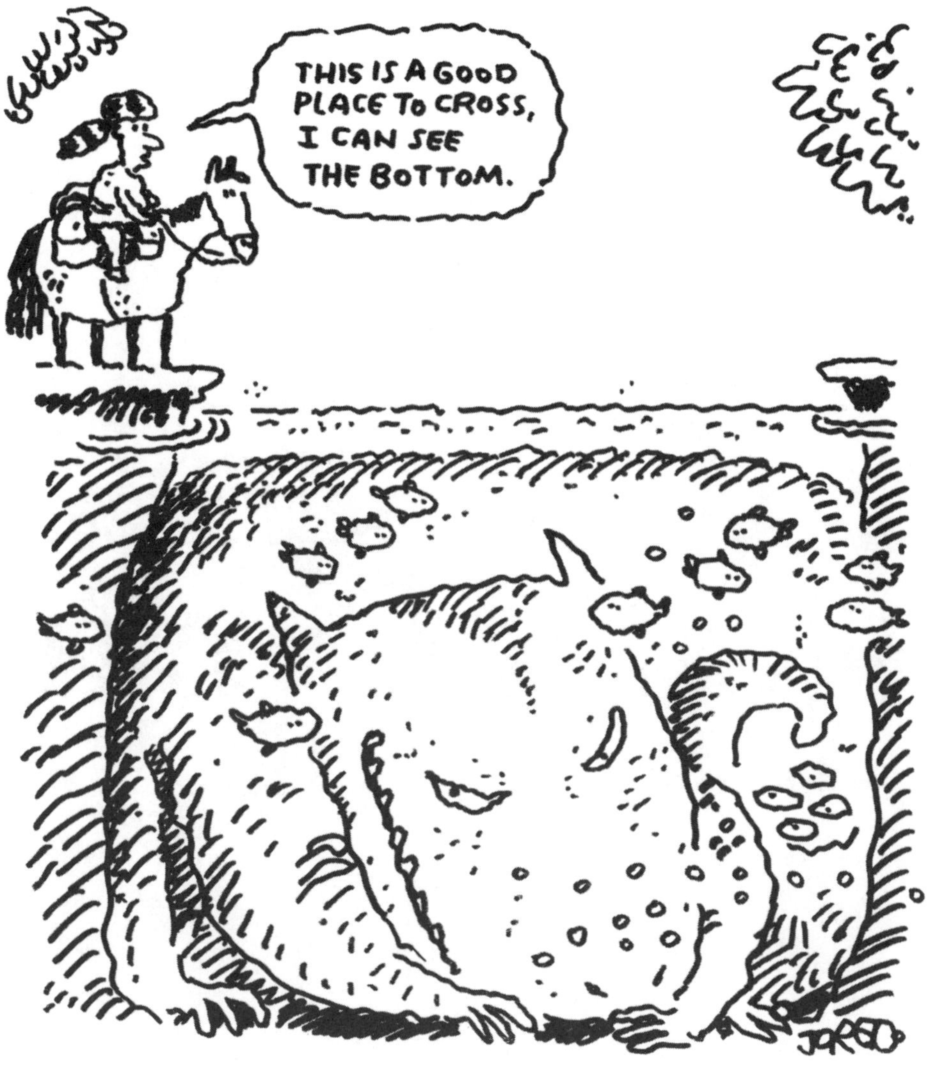
THIS IS A GOOD PLACE TO CROSS, I CAN SEE THE BOTTOM.
JARED

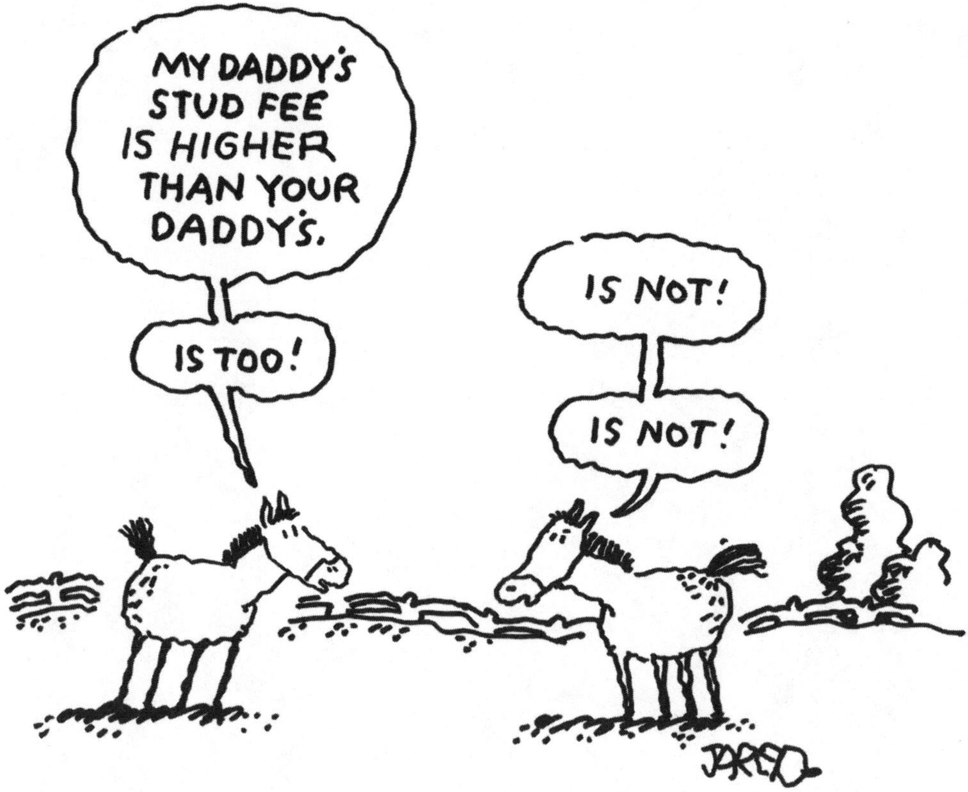
MY DADDY'S STUD FEE IS HIGHER THAN YOUR DADDY'S.
IS TOO!
IS NOT!
IS NOT!
JARED

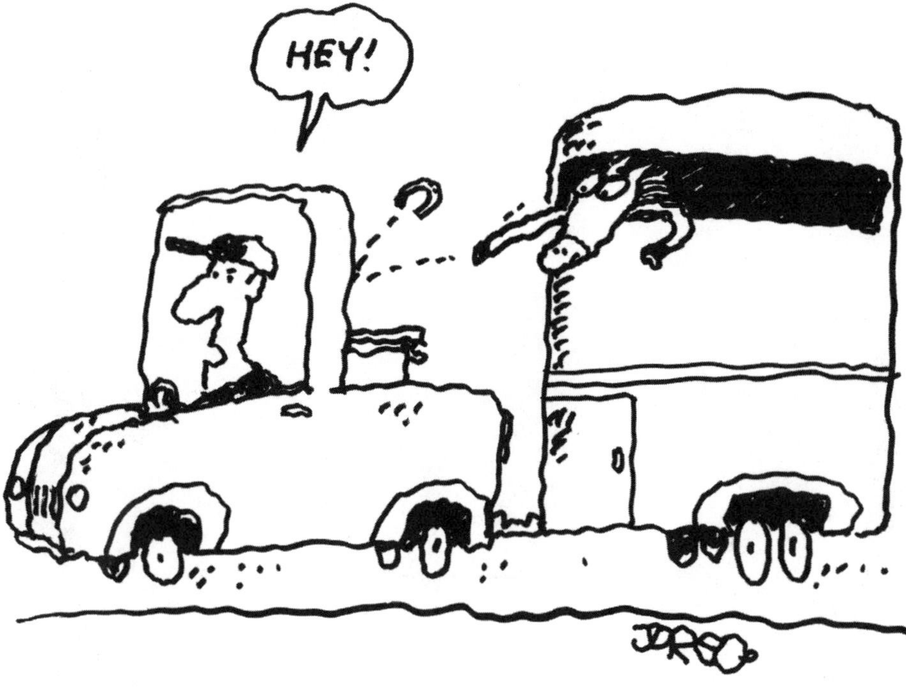
HEY!

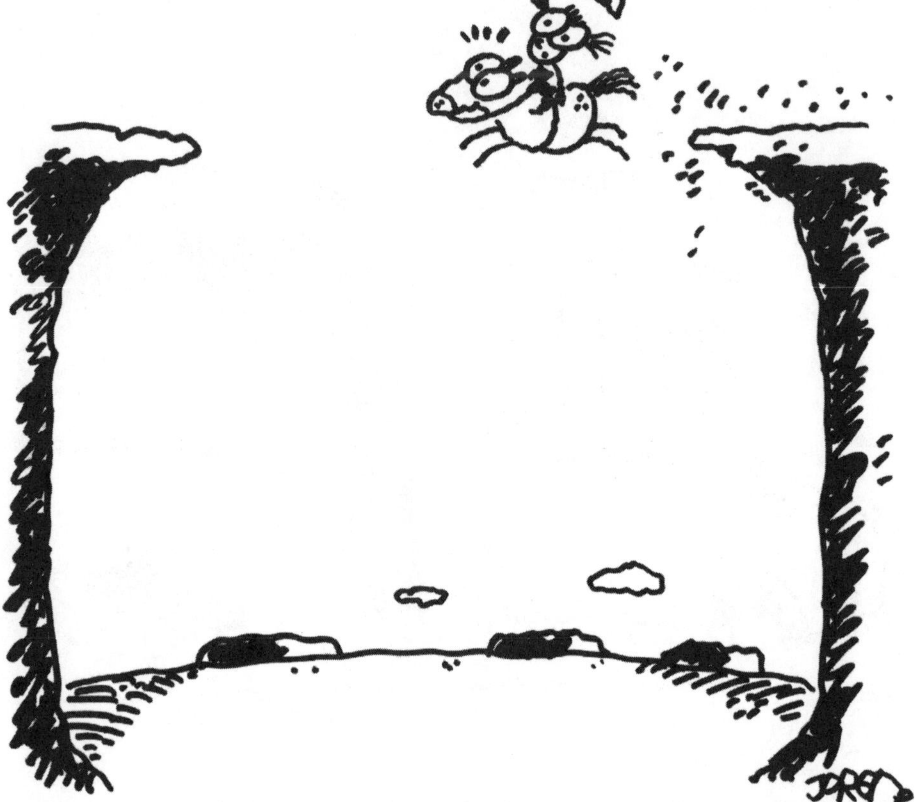

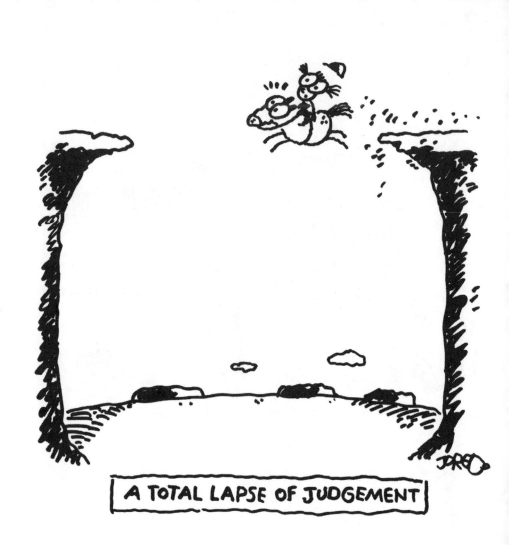

A TOTAL LAPSE OF JUDGEMENT

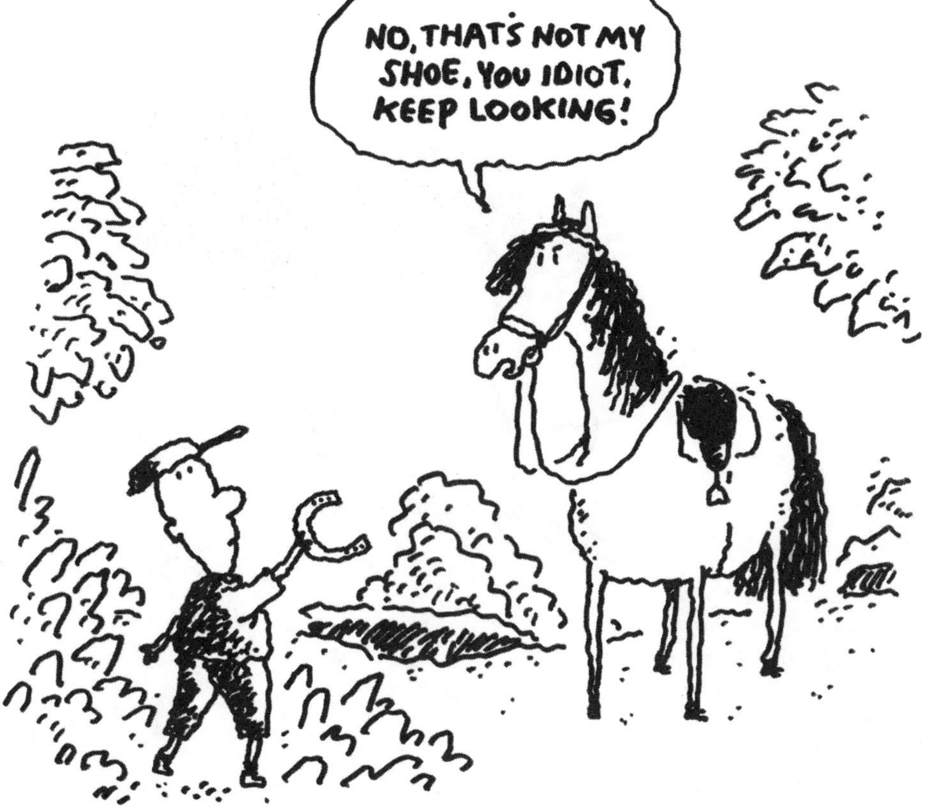
NO, THAT'S NOT MY SHOE, YOU IDIOT. KEEP LOOKING!

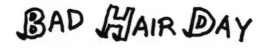

BAD HAIR DAY

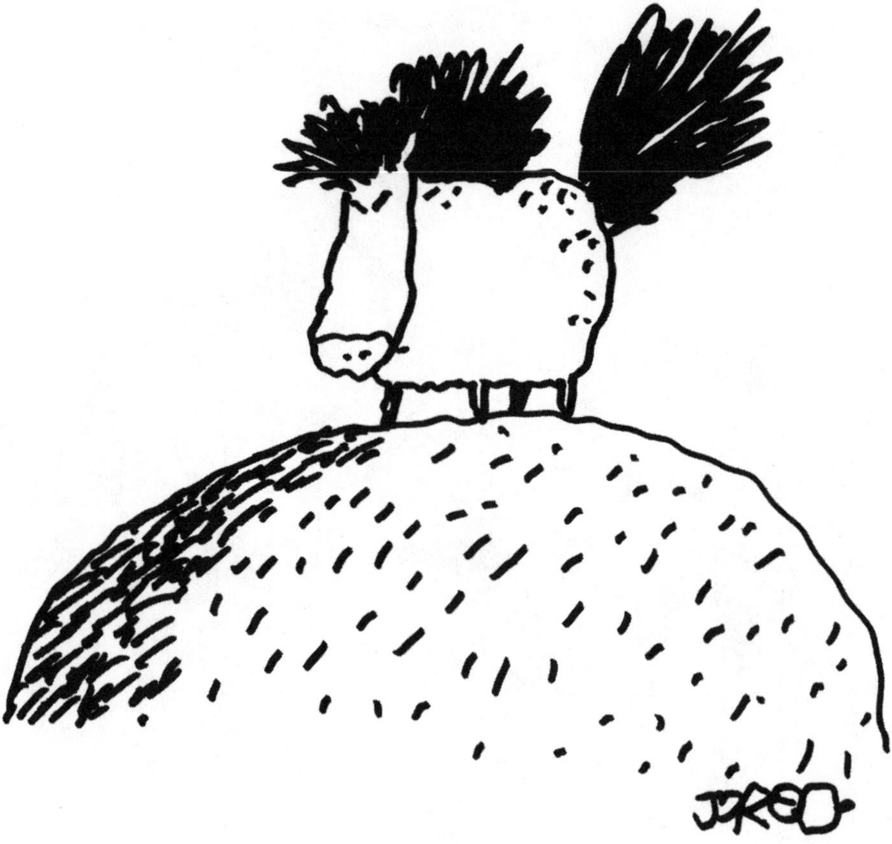

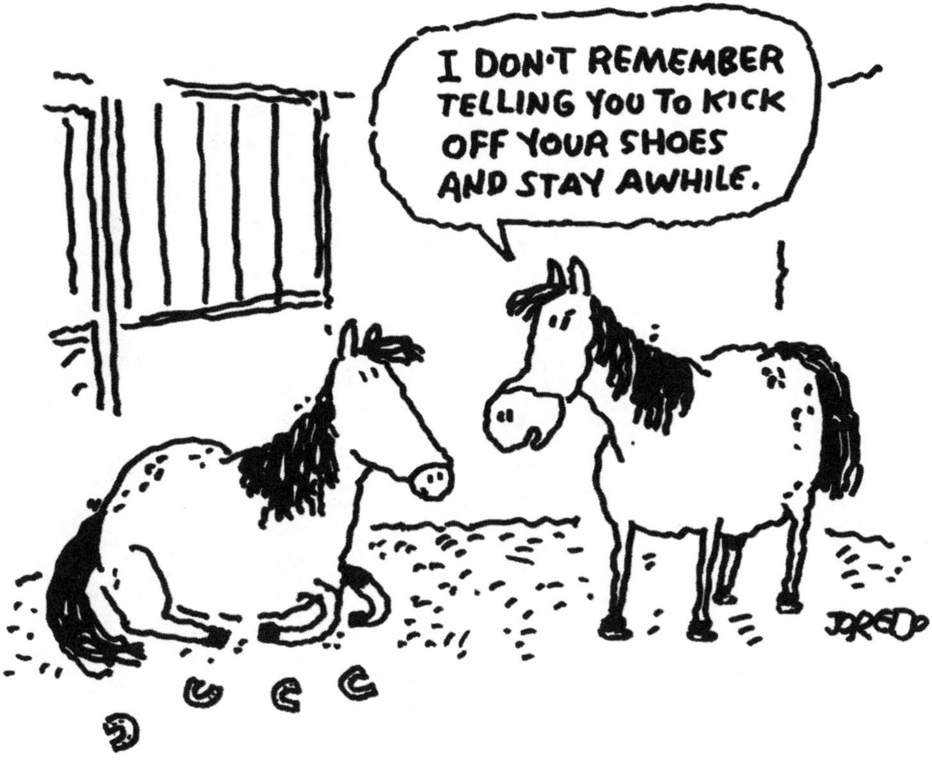
I DON'T REMEMBER TELLING YOU TO KICK OFF YOUR SHOES AND STAY AWHILE.
JORDO

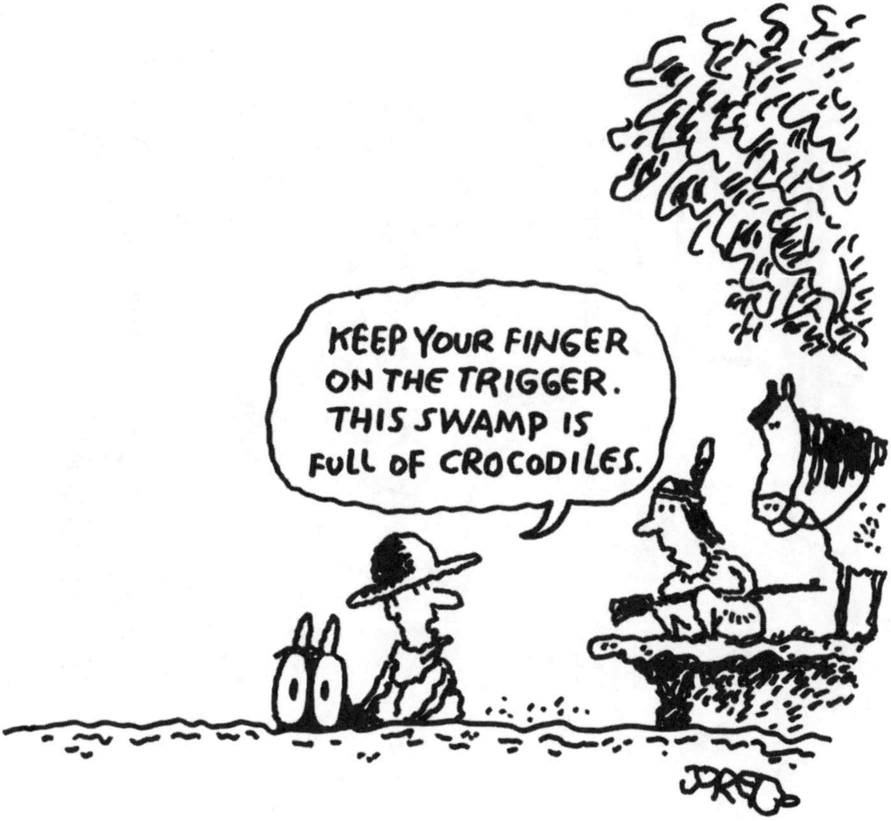
KEEP YOUR FINGER ON THE TRIGGER. THIS SWAMP IS FULL OF CROCODILES.
JOREO

THE DYSLEXIC RIDER

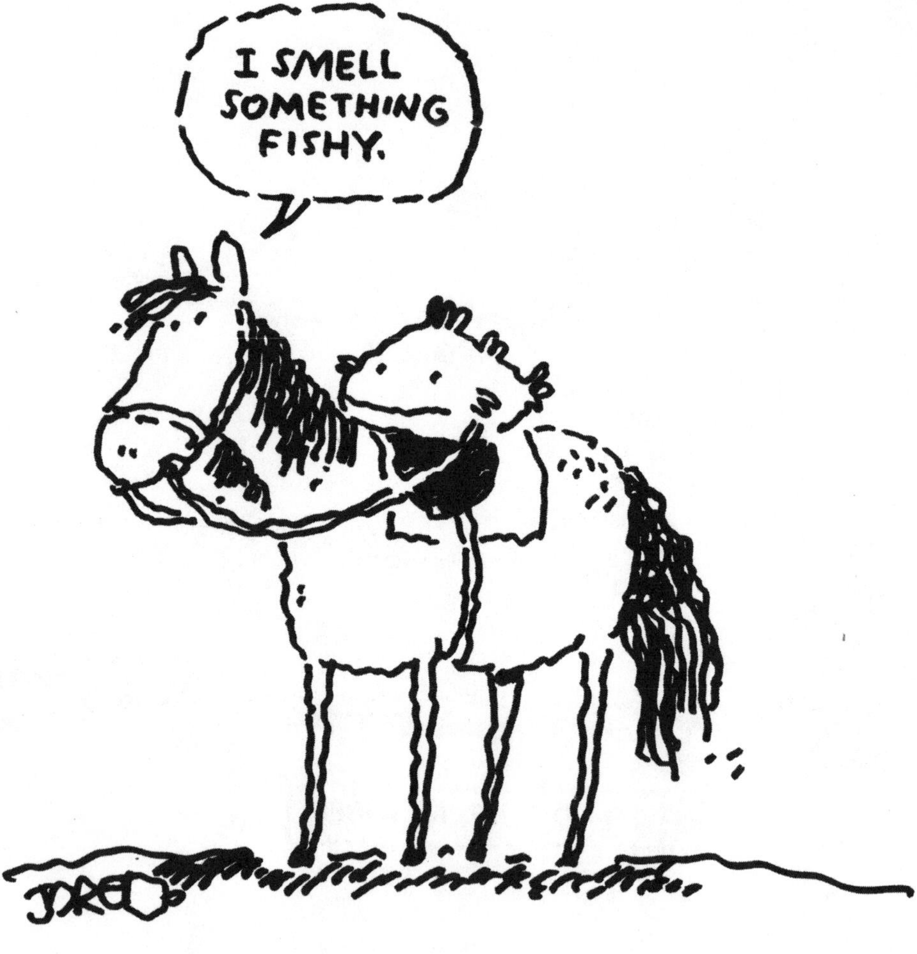
I SMELL SOMETHING FISHY.
JOREO

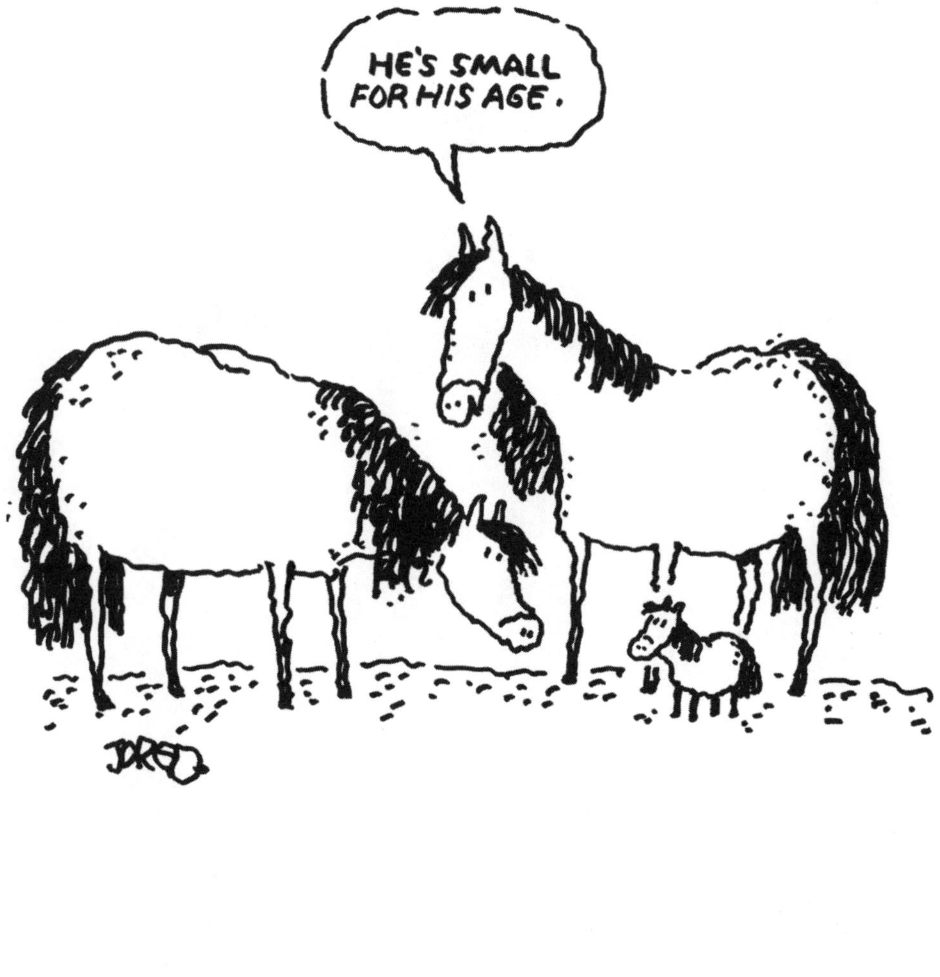
HE'S SMALL
FOR HIS AGE.
JDREED

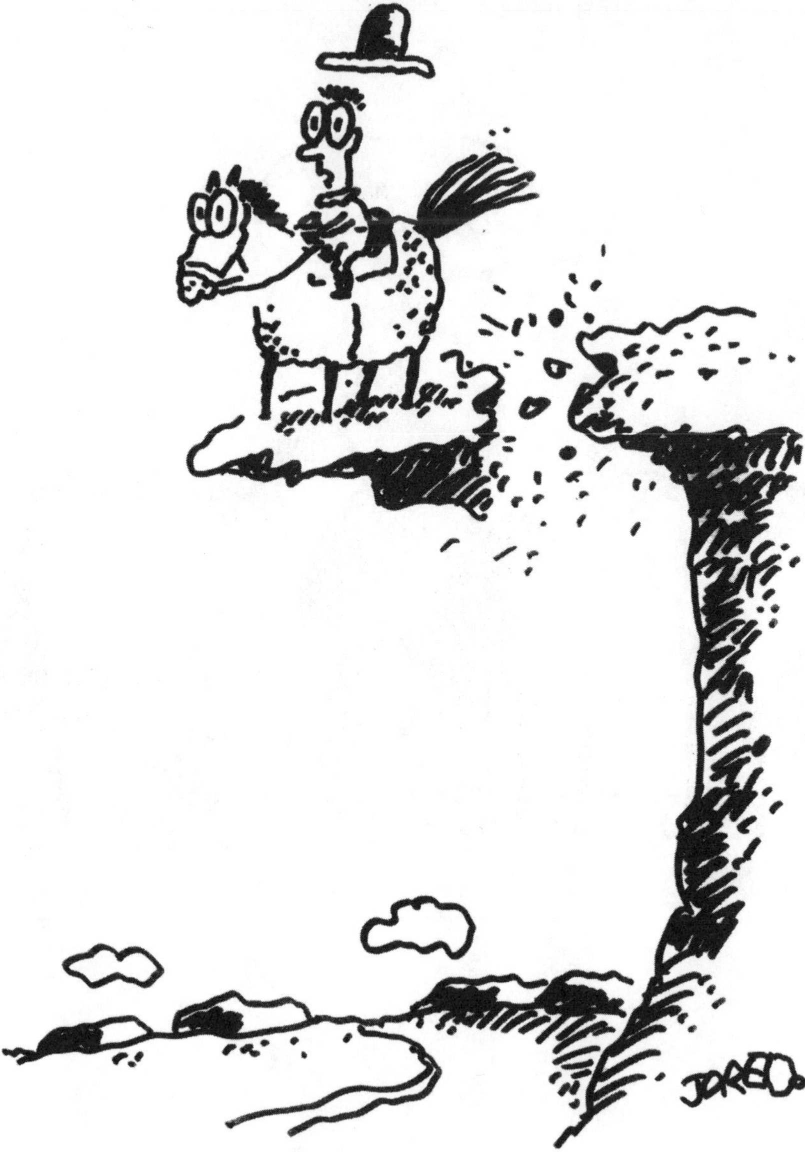
JOREO.

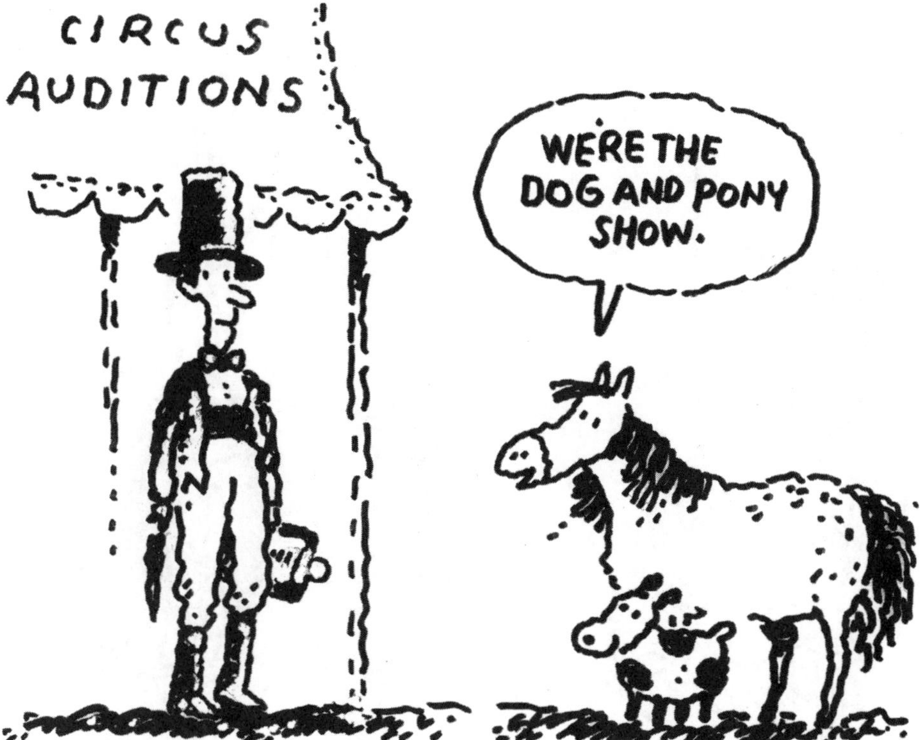
CIRCUS AUDITIONS
WE'RE THE DOG AND PONY SHOW.
JARED

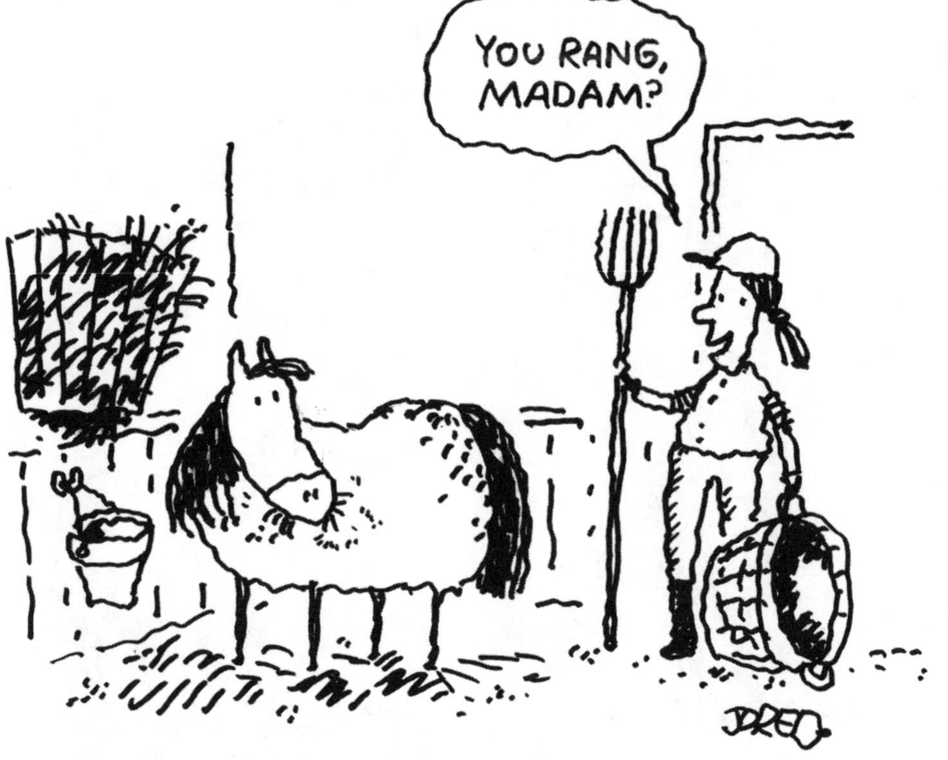
YOU RANG, MADAM?
JOREO

EASY RIDER

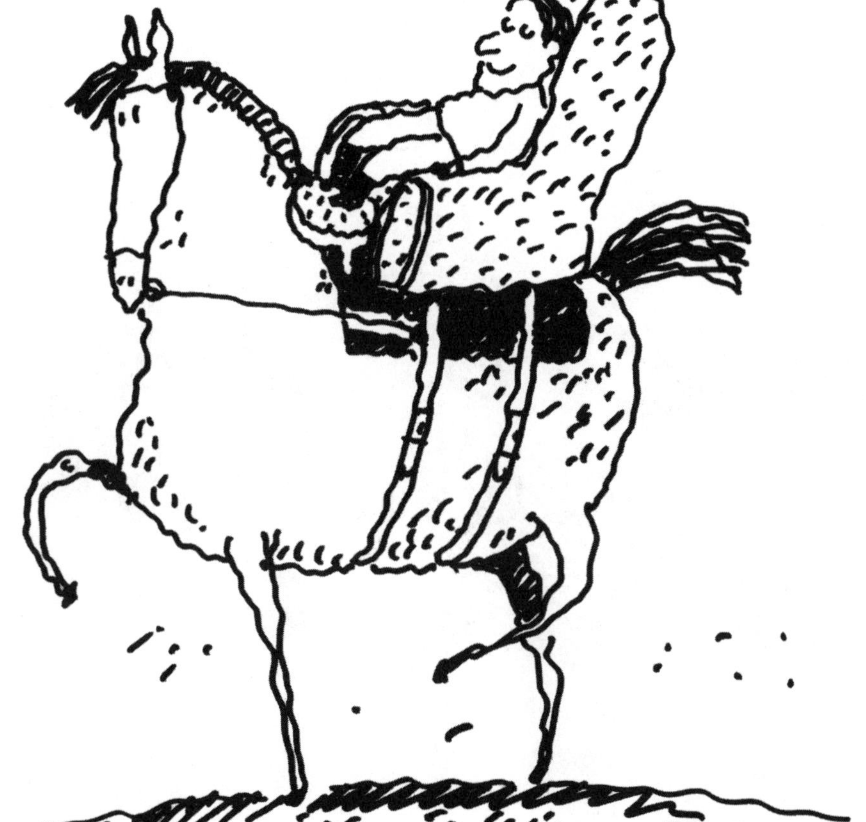

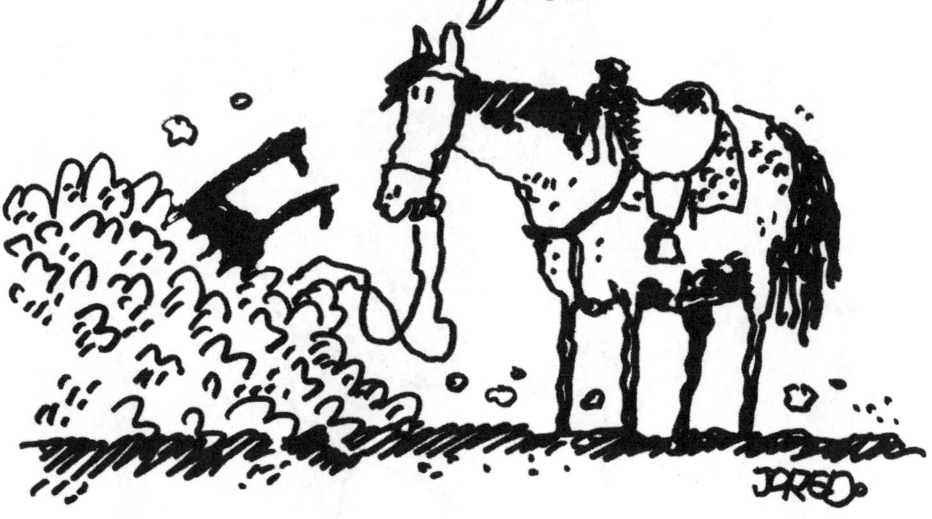
WHAT MAKES YOU THINK I DON'T LIKE YOU?
JARED

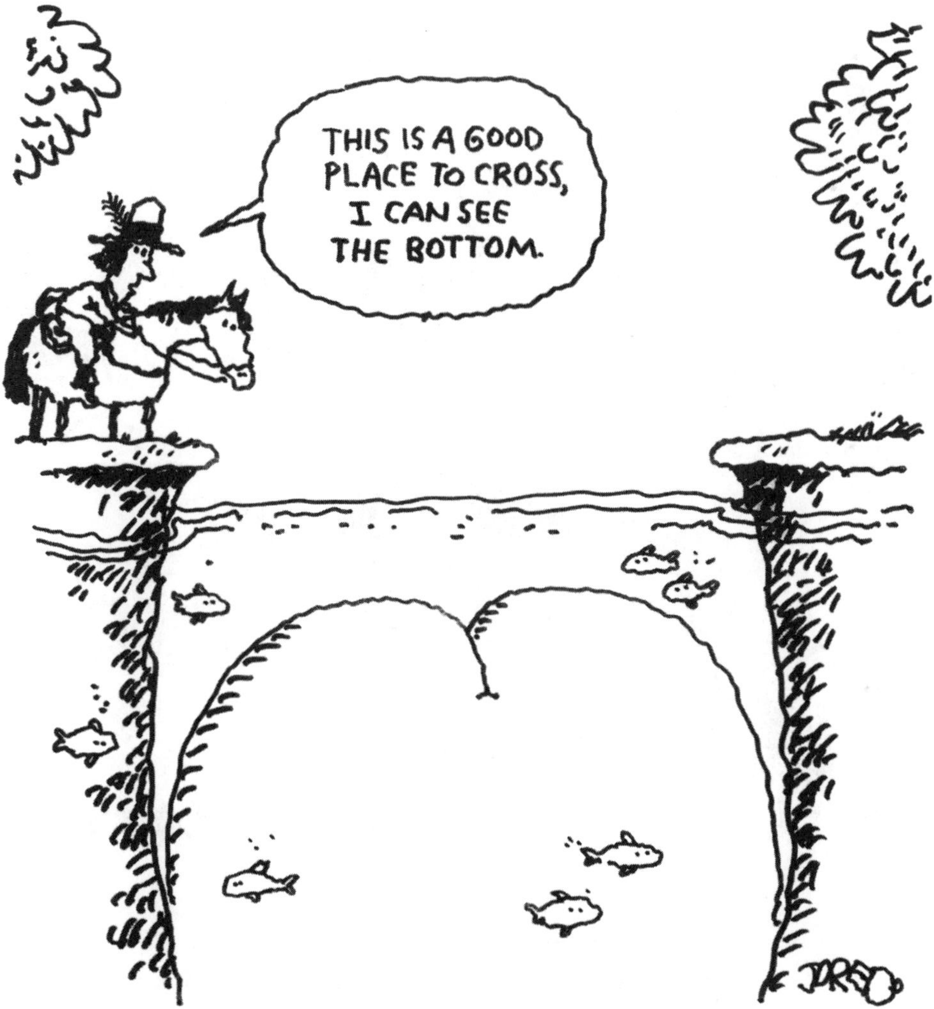
THIS IS A GOOD PLACE TO CROSS, I CAN SEE THE BOTTOM.
JOREO

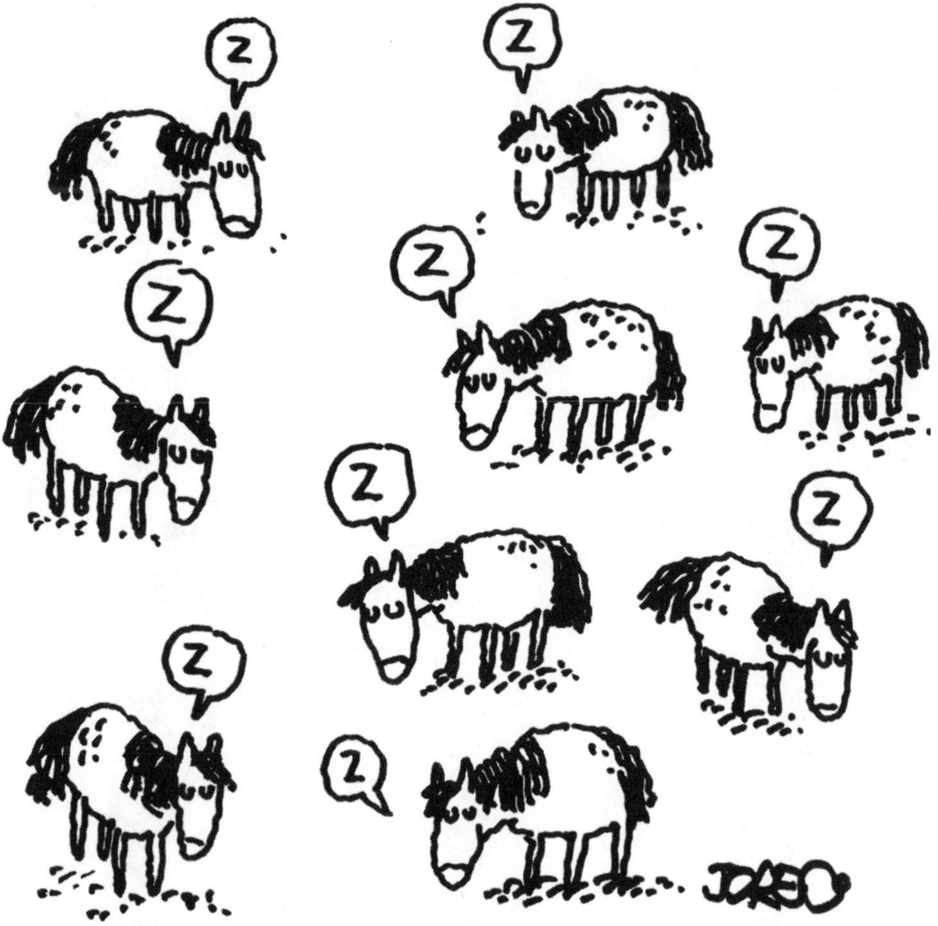
Z
Z
Z
Z
Z
Z
Z
Z
Z
Z

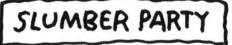

SLUMBER PARTY

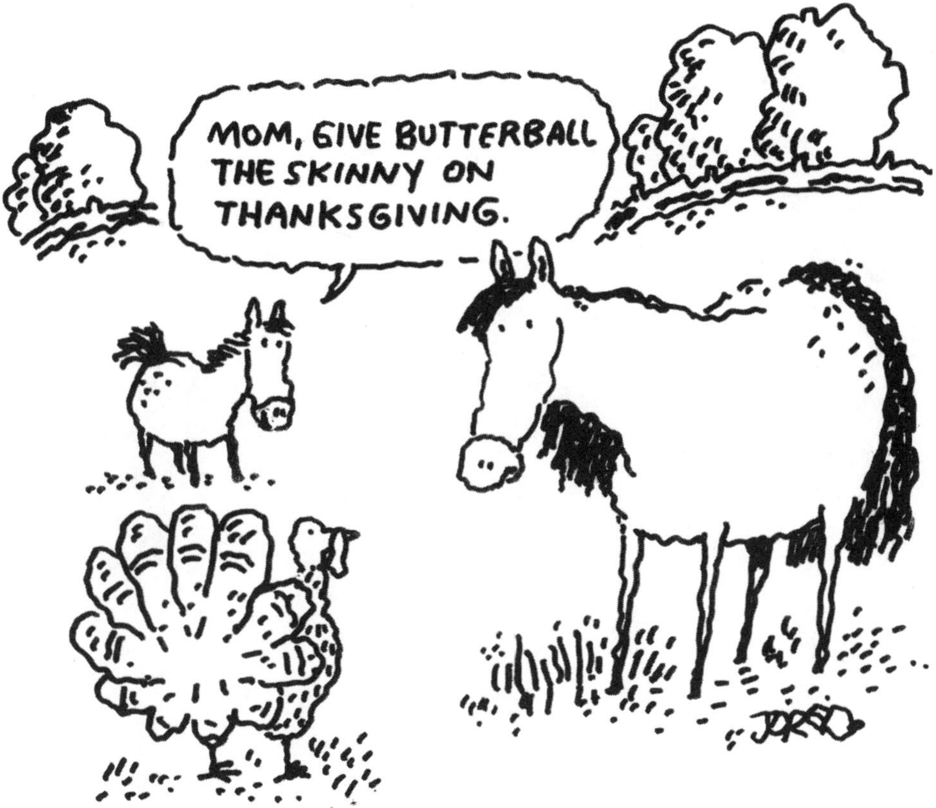
MOM, GIVE BUTTERBALL THE SKINNY ON THANKSGIVING.
JARED

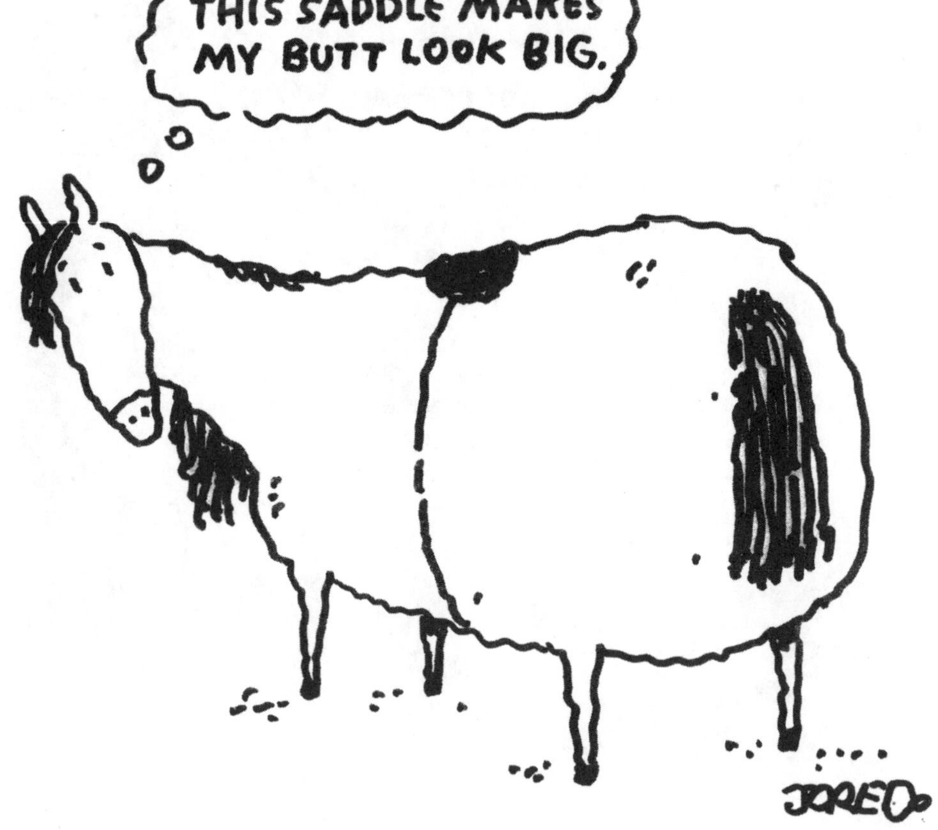
THIS SADDLE MAKES MY BUTT LOOK BIG.
JARED

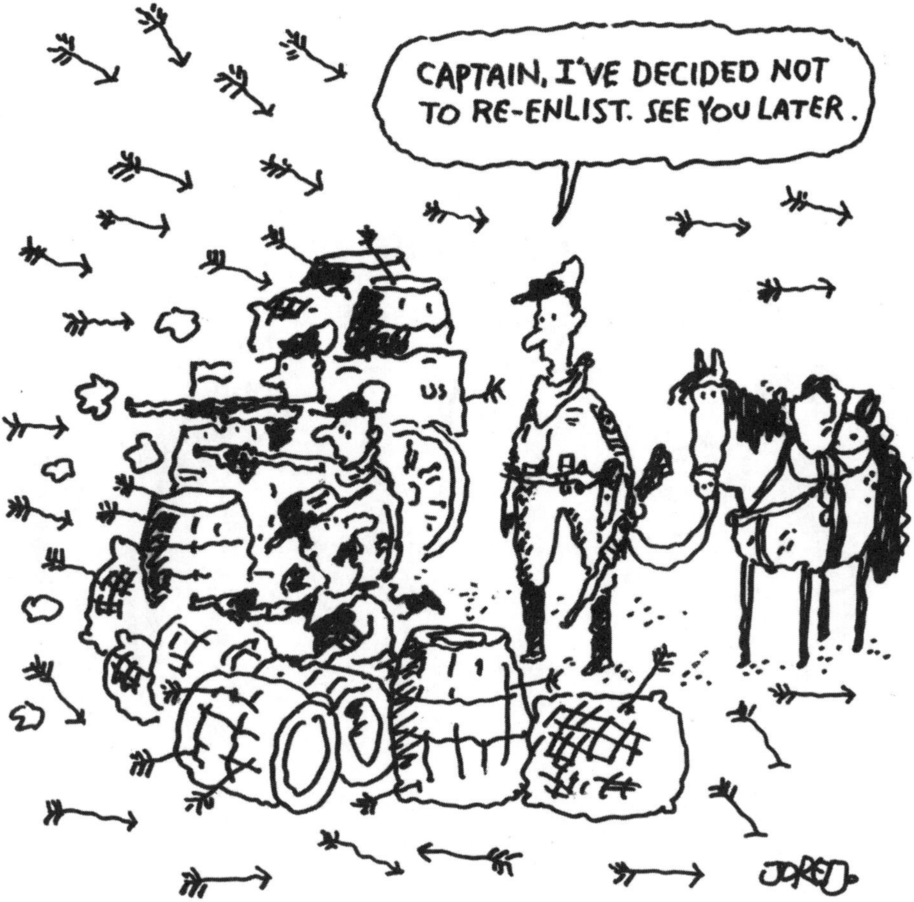
CAPTAIN, I'VE DECIDED NOT TO RE-ENLIST. SEE YOU LATER.
US
JORED

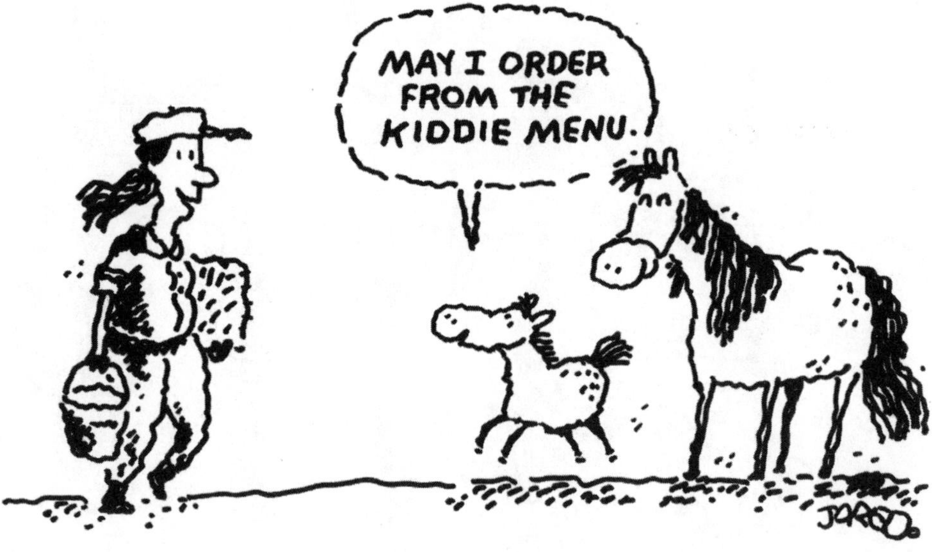
MAY I ORDER FROM THE KIDDIE MENU.
JARED

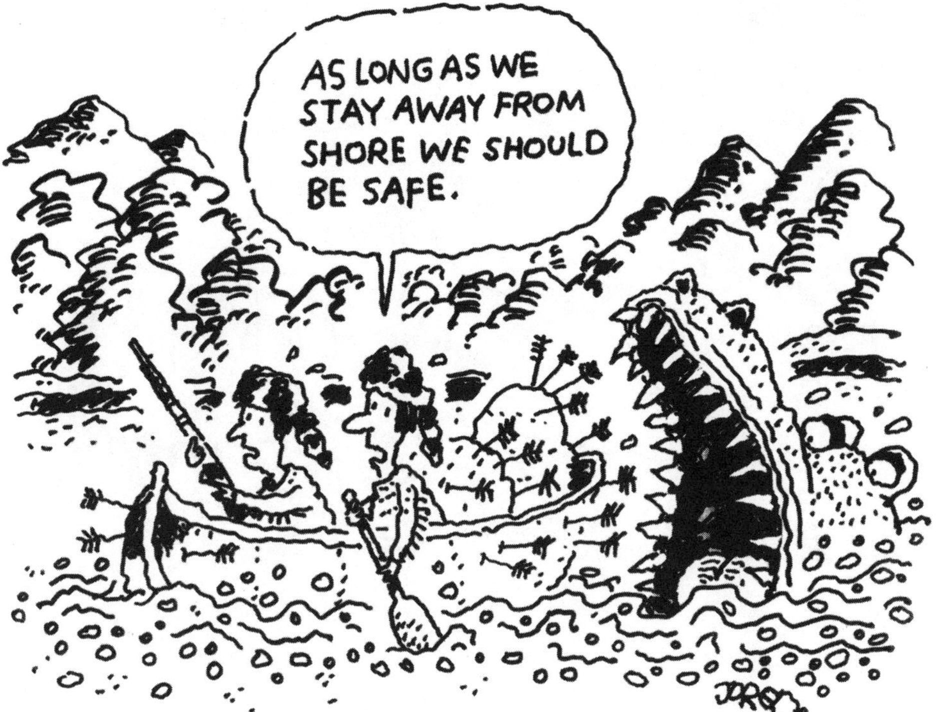
AS LONG AS WE STAY AWAY FROM SHORE WE SHOULD BE SAFE.
JDRE

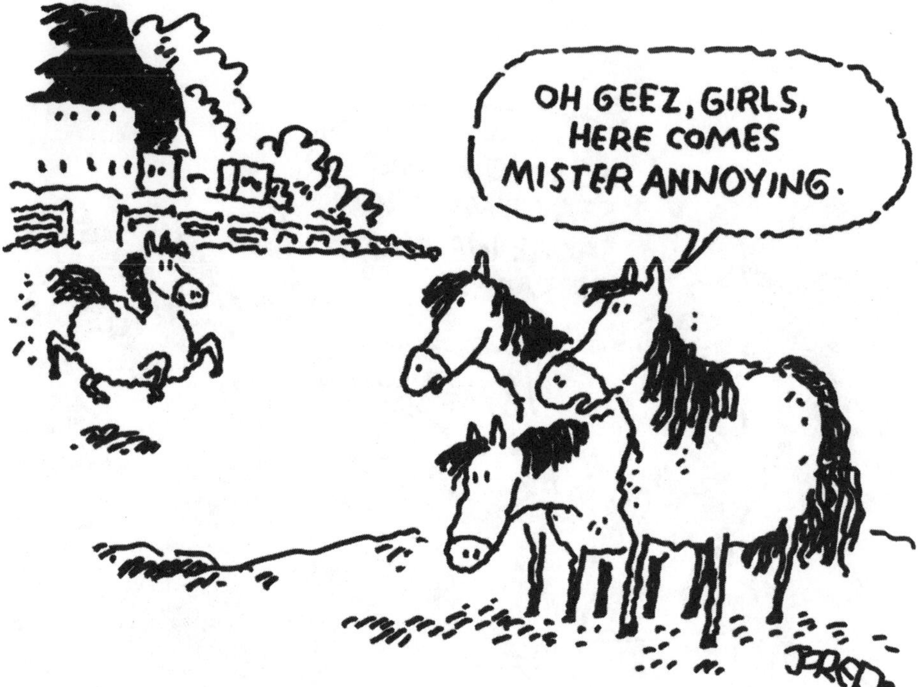
OH GEEZ, GIRLS, HERE COMES MISTER ANNOYING.
JARED

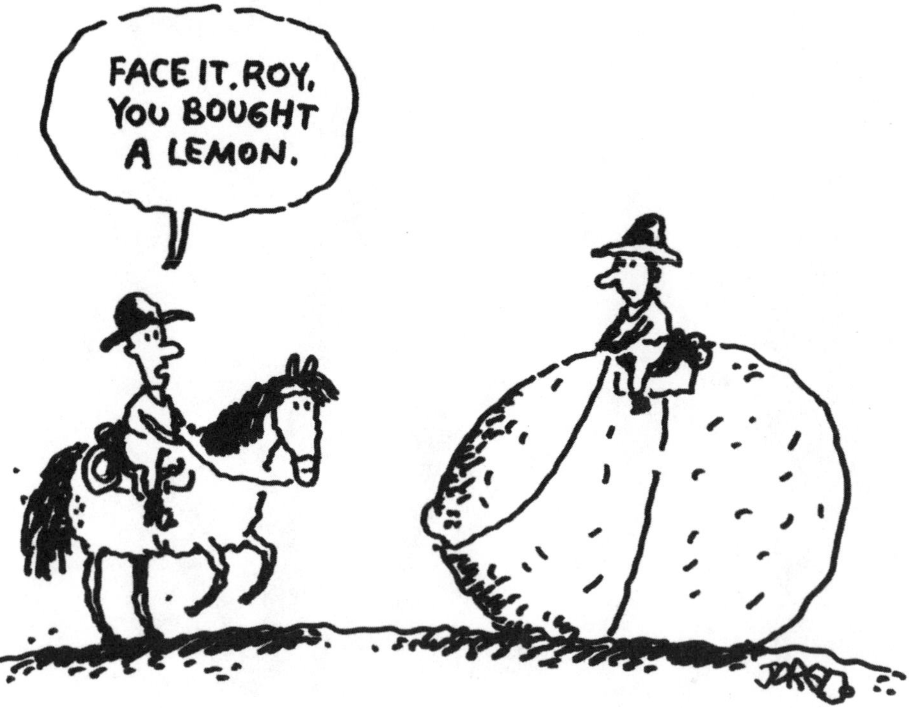
FACE IT, ROY, YOU BOUGHT A LEMON.

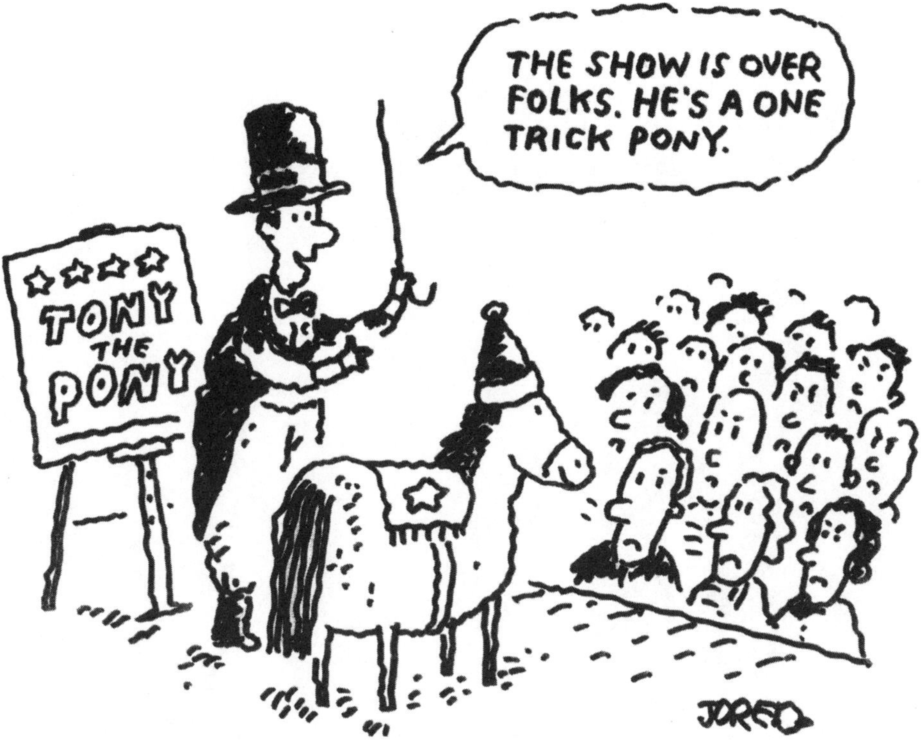
THE SHOW IS OVER FOLKS. HE'S A ONE TRICK PONY.
TONY THE PONY
JORGO

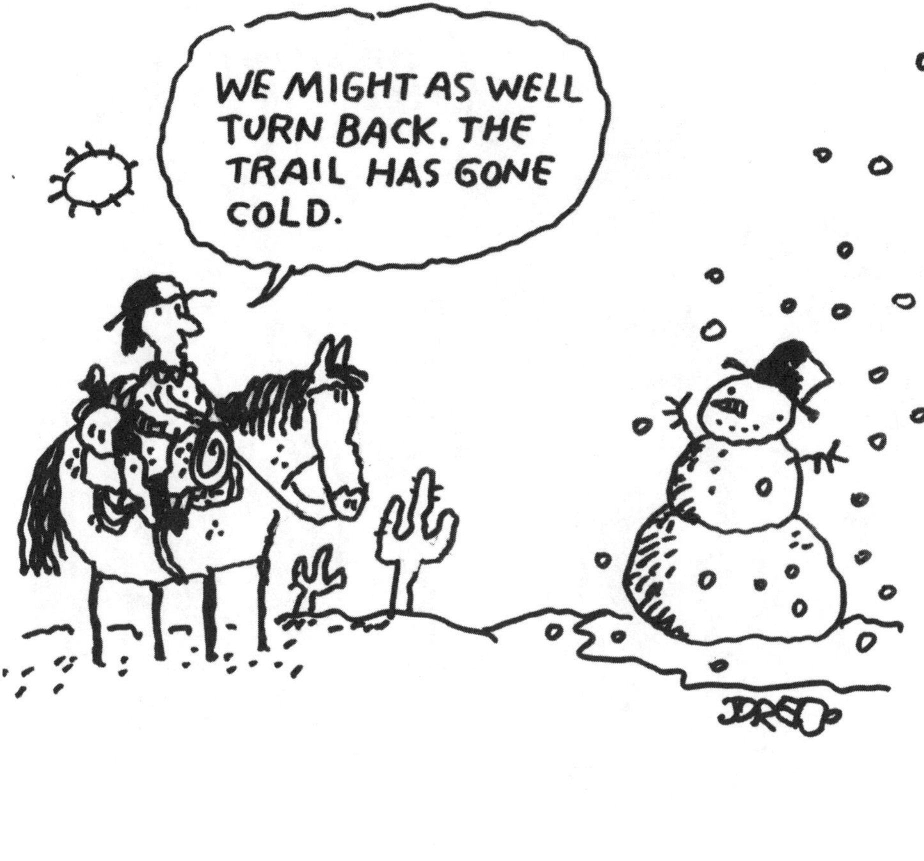
WE MIGHT AS WELL TURN BACK. THE TRAIL HAS GONE COLD.
JDRED

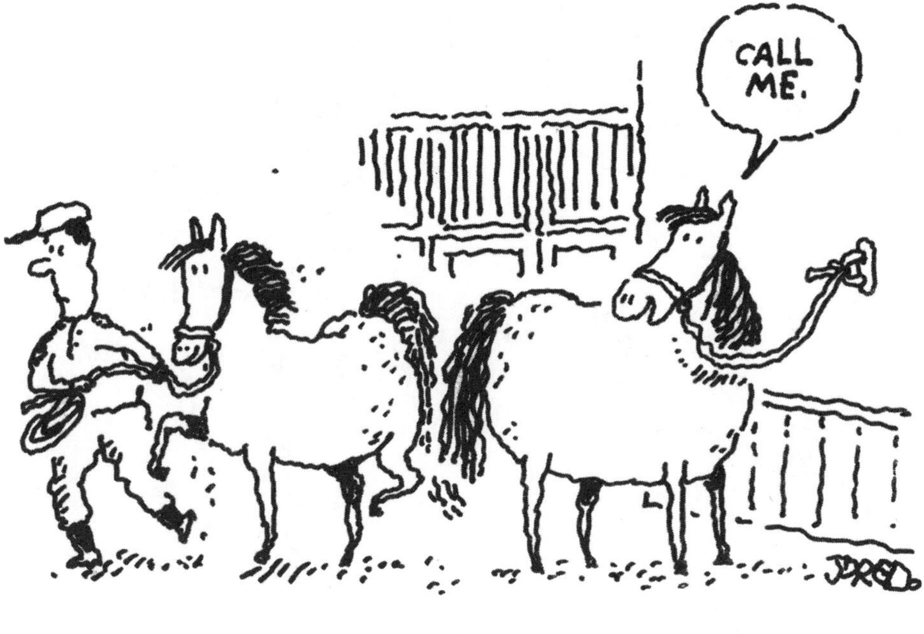
CALL ME.
JDRED

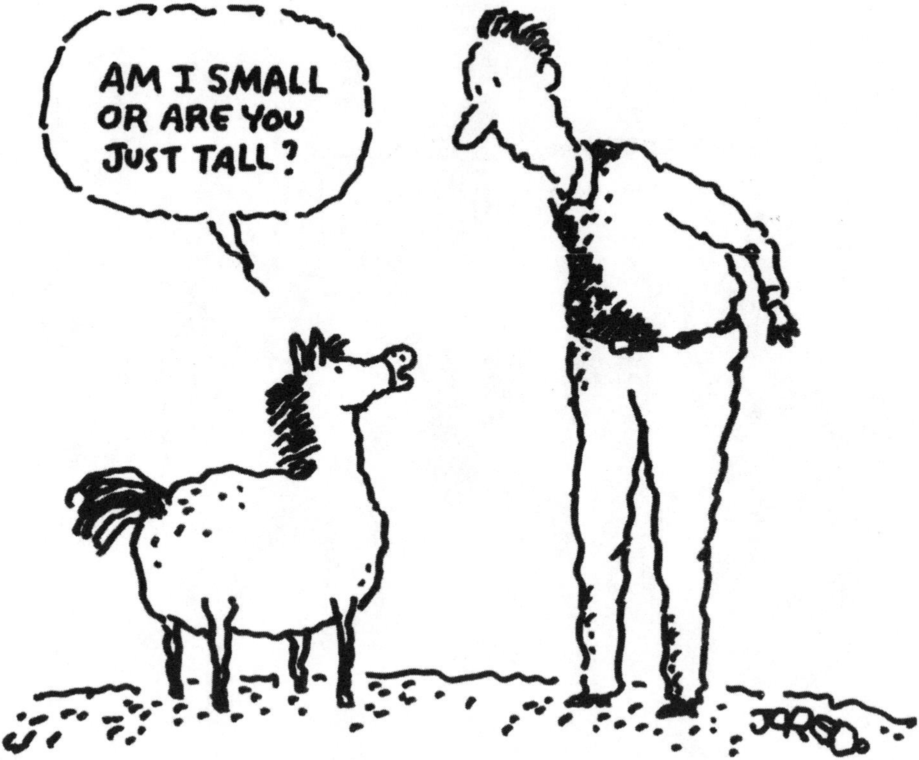
AM I SMALL OR ARE YOU JUST TALL?
JARSO

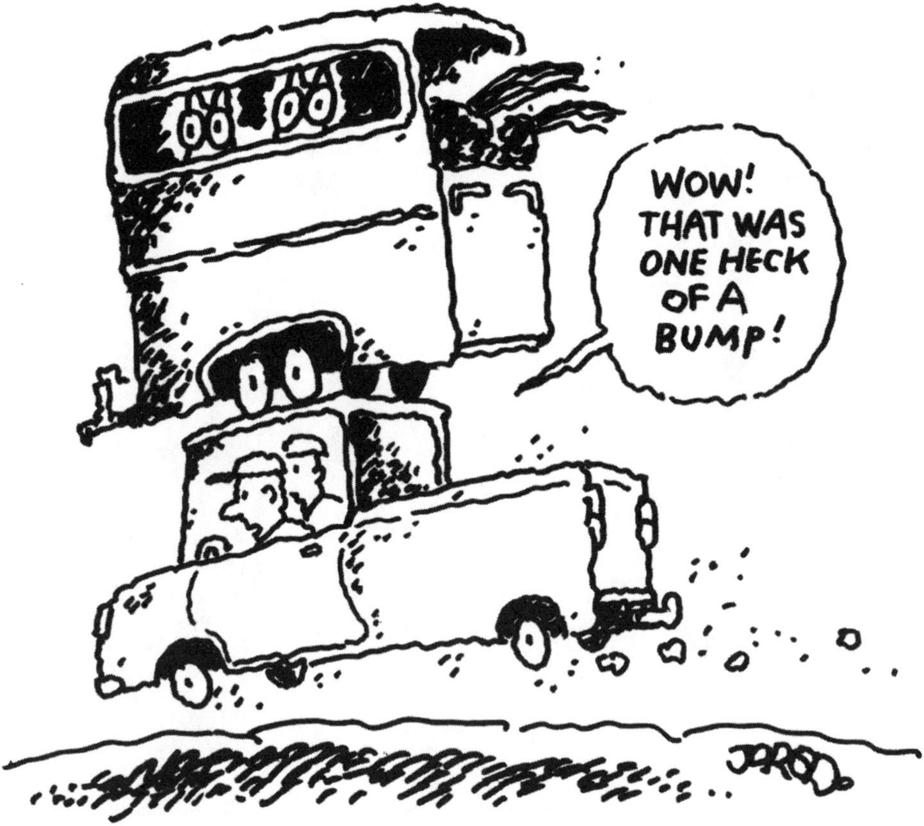
WOW! THAT WAS ONE HECK OF A BUMP!
JARED

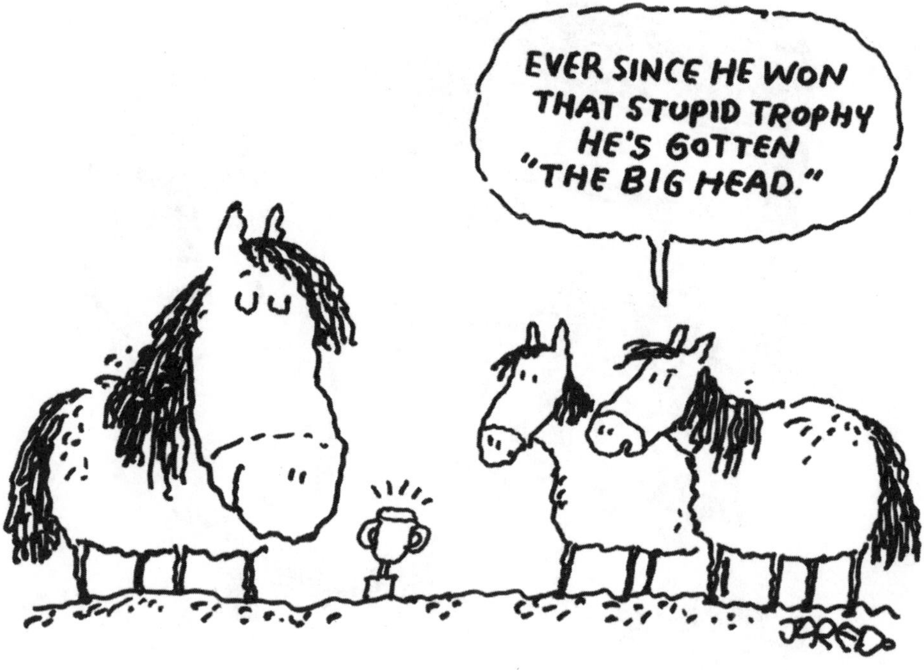
EVER SINCE HE WON THAT STUPID TROPHY HE'S GOTTEN "THE BIG HEAD."
JARED

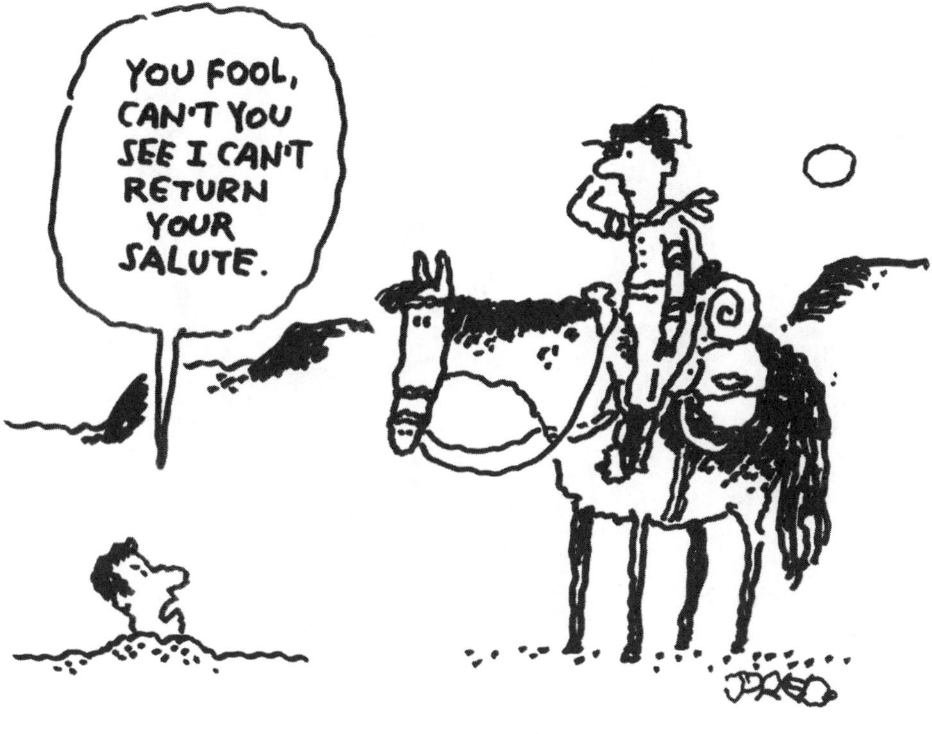
YOU FOOL, CAN'T YOU SEE I CAN'T RETURN YOUR SALUTE.

HOLD YOUR HORSES

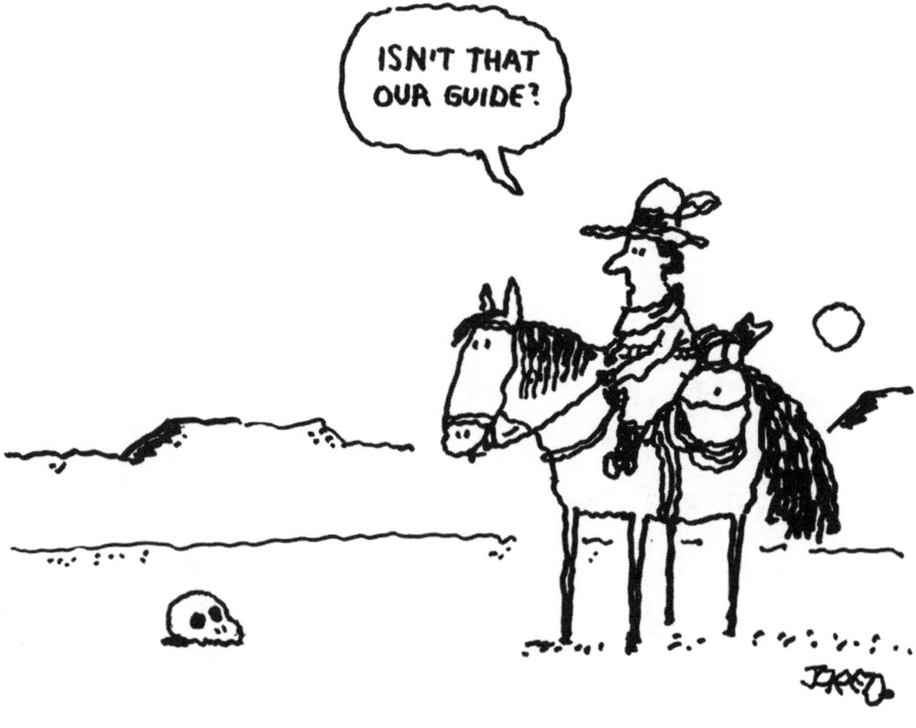
ISN'T THAT OUR GUIDE?
JARED

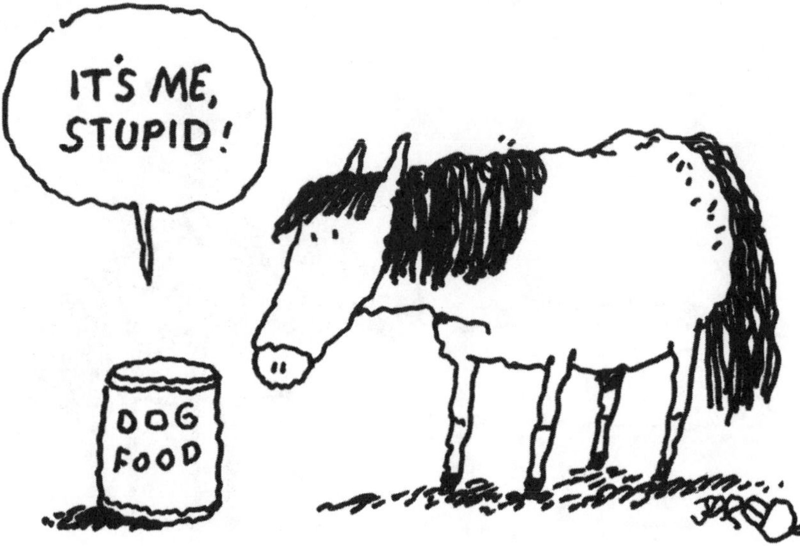
IT'S ME, STUPID!
DOG FOOD

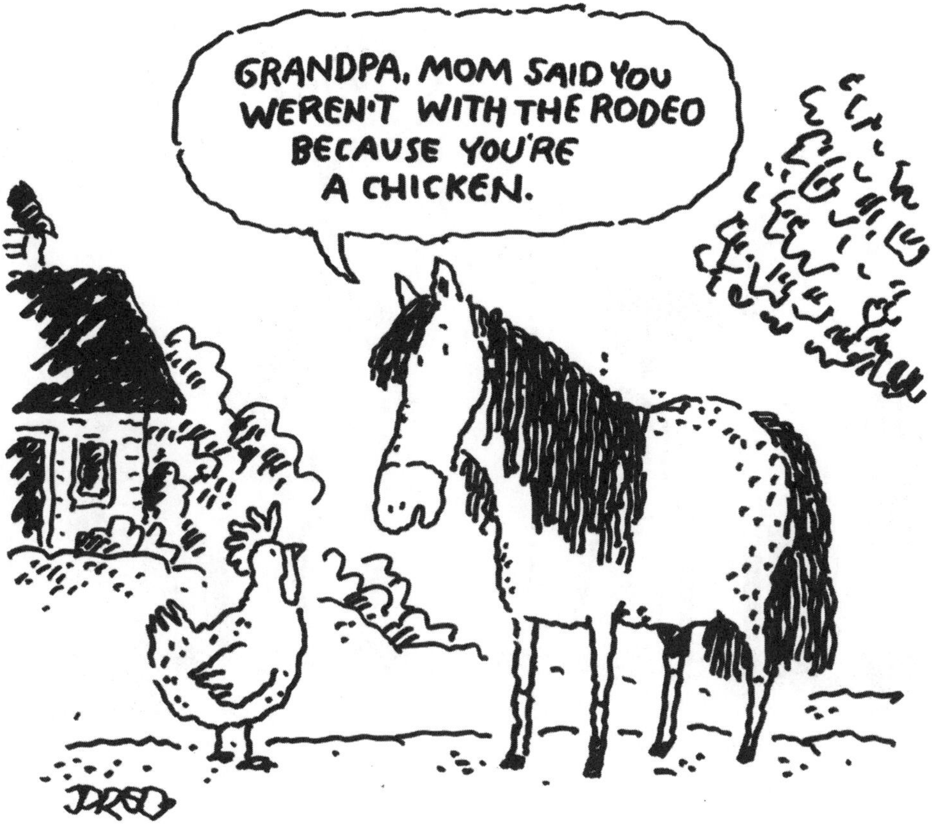
GRANDPA, MOM SAID YOU WEREN'T WITH THE RODEO BECAUSE YOU'RE A CHICKEN.
JDREO

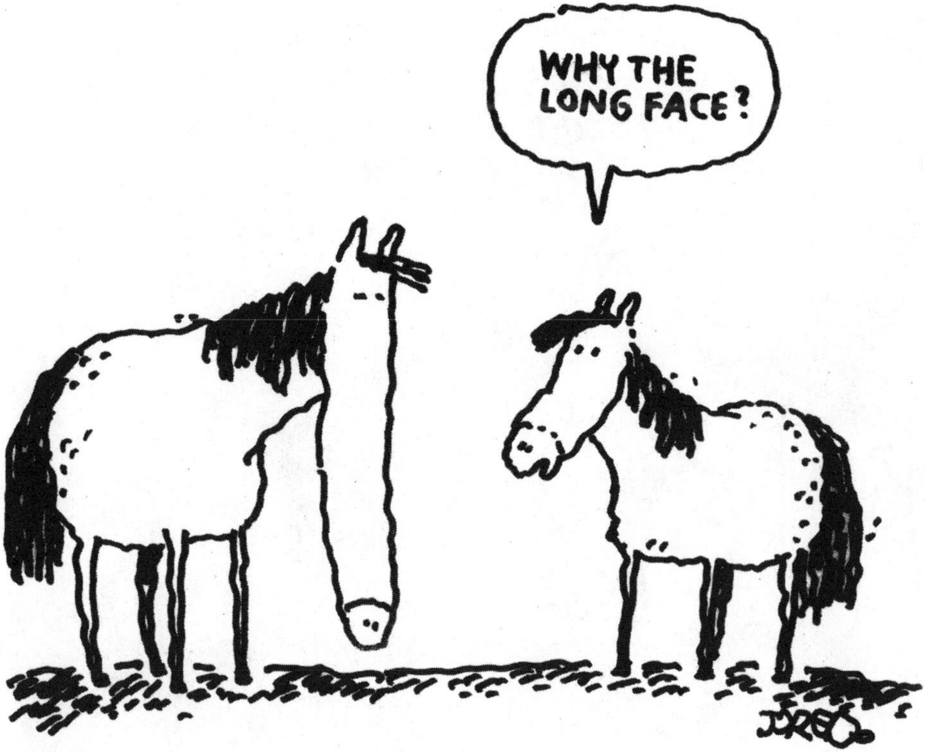
WHY THE LONG FACE?

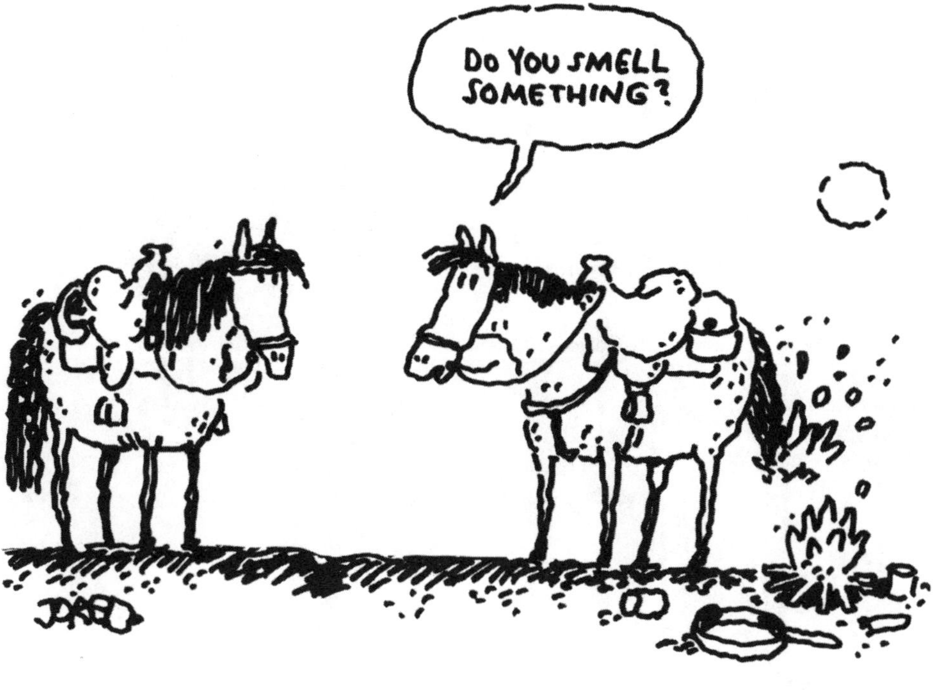
DO YOU SMELL SOMETHING?

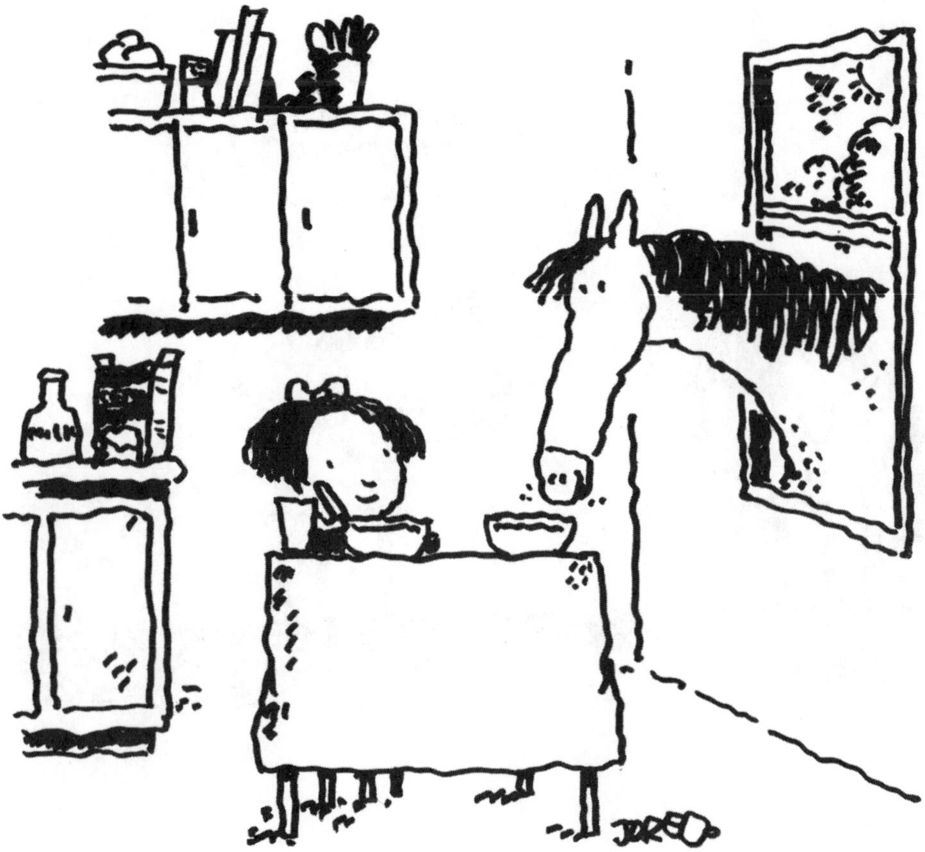

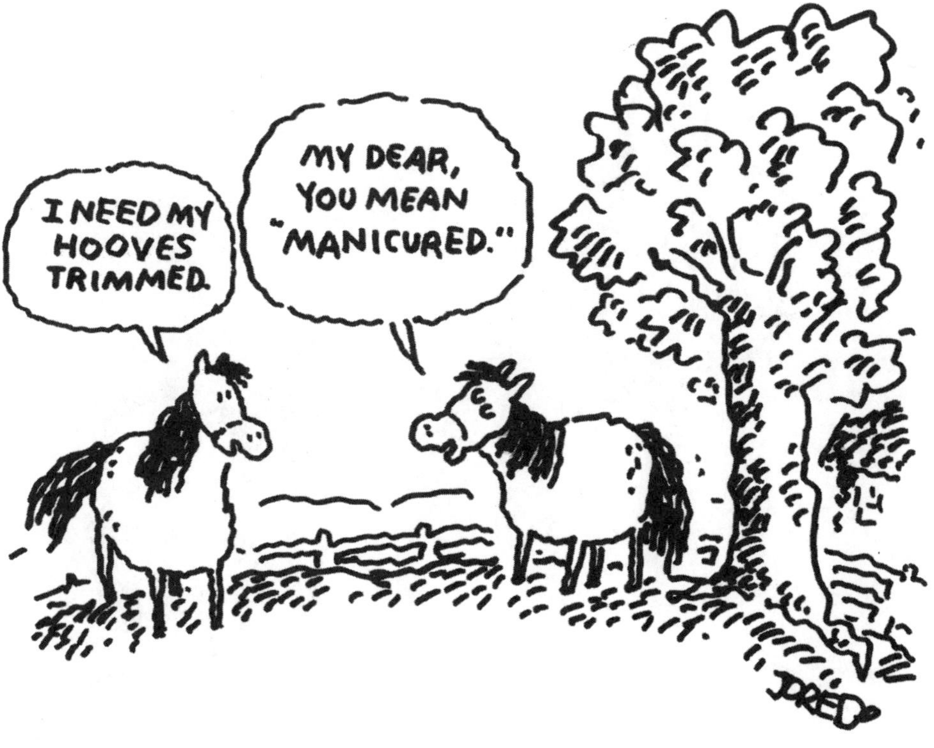
I NEED MY HOOVES TRIMMED.
MY DEAR, YOU MEAN "MANICURED."
JORRED

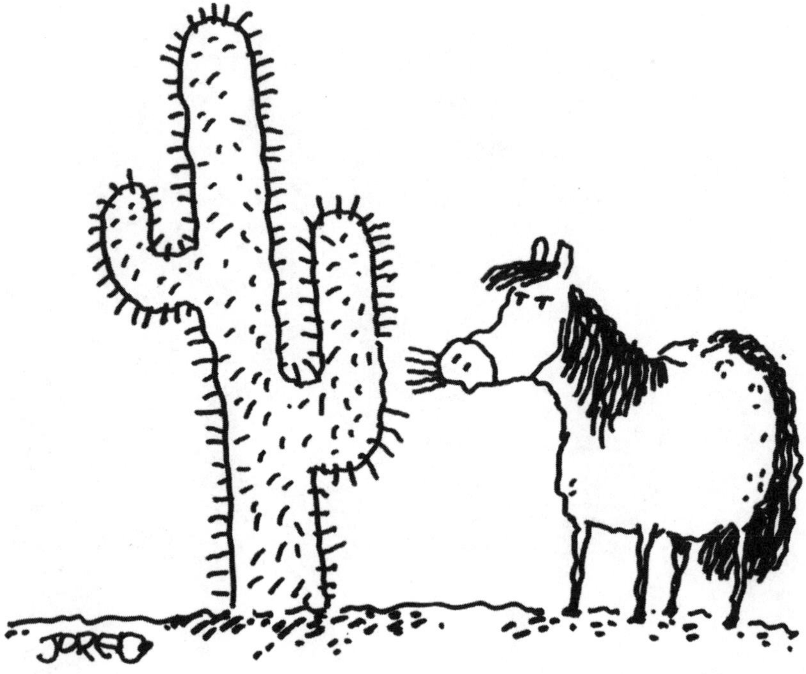
JORED